FROM CUPCAKES TO CHEMICALS

FROM CUPCAKES TO CHEMICALS

HOW THE CULTURE OF ALARMISM MAKES US AFRAID OF EVERYTHING AND HOW TO FIGHT BACK

JULIE GUNLOCK

From Cupcakes to Chemicals: How the Culture of Alarmism
Makes Us Afraid of Everything — and How to Fight Back
by Julie Gunlock

Pubished by IWF Press
ISBN-13: 978-0615906904
ISBN-10: 0615906907

Book Design by Sekayi A. Stephens

DEDICATION

To Darren, who makes me feel safe every day.
And to my three brave boys: Jack, Henry, and Willie.

TABLE OF CONTENTS

. . . .

INTRODUCTION ix

PART I
THE MEDIA, ACTIVISTS, AND GOVERNMENT –
HOW AND WHY THEY WANT YOU SCARED!

CHAPTER 1
The Cycle of Alarmism 3

CHAPTER 2
Be Afraid...of Everything! 17

CHAPTER 3
Your Lesser Angels Will Always Win 25

PART II
THE MISUSE OF SCIENCE

CHAPTER 4
Mom's Guide to Good Science 37

CHAPTER 5
Studies Say... 51

CHAPTER 6
The Danger of Fickle Science
(or Is Anyone Listening Anymore?) 65

PART III
THE EXPENSIVE "SOLUTIONS" TO ALARMISM

CHAPTER 7
Our Obese Government Is Gobbling Us Up   75

CHAPTER 8
Scaring Away Safe and Healthy Products   83

CHAPTER 9
The High Costs to Businesses and Jobs   97

PART IV
HOW TO RECOGNIZE AND FIGHT BACK AGAINST ALARMISM

CHAPTER 10
Fighting Fear   109

ENDNOTES   123

ABOUT THE AUTHOR   135

ABOUT THE INDEPENDENT WOMEN'S FORUM   137

INTRODUCTION

. . . .

My life changed dramatically after my son was born. In addition to the obvious changes that come with having a child and becoming a mother, I found my interests evolving as well.

With a little extra time on my hands due to my decision to stay home rather than return to work right away, I began gravitating toward mommy and women-centric blogs, parenting websites, television shows focusing on health and wellness, home decorating books and magazines, and what I call "how to be perfect" websites. Topics I found somewhat boring and pretentious pre-baby (who cares about how to make flawless bumblebee cupcakes!) suddenly seemed useful and entertaining as I assumed my new role.

Yet, the more I read and watched, the more I also felt like I'd fallen down the rabbit hole with Alice.

I had entered an entirely new world—one I didn't really like, one in which I didn't feel entirely safe, one that, at times, I wished I could escape. But the draw was also difficult to deny. These websites, magazines, and television shows all had something in common—they often drifted into promoting a message of fear and alarmism, warning that the world was a dangerous, unhealthy place.

I was already quite adept at creating my own scary thoughts. I worried constantly that I wasn't a good enough mother, that my child wouldn't receive enough stimulation, that he wouldn't become all that he could be because of my mistakes, that he'd become sick or harmed in some lasting way. Like an adrenalin junkie, I gravitated to the sources that fed my fears and anxieties. These sites supported my self-flagellating mantra that I could do more, more, more!

I was warned that normal, everyday activities, food, and products were dangerous for my family. I was told to throw out the very items that, frankly, were making my life a whole lot easier—like my baby swing, my trusty household cleaners (many of which I'd seen my own mother use when I was a child), plastic food containers, the crib mattress and mattress pad, even the bedding I'd selected ("crib bumpers are killers!"), my garden hose, my child's sippy cups and toys, even certain foods that my son loved. I felt like everything was being portrayed as a potential threat.

Of course, while I was shocked and horrified by what I was reading, I was also inspired. It sounds cliché, but I wasn't just interested in being just a good mom: I was going to be the best mom. Doing right by my son gave me a sense of purpose and made me feel like superwoman in my role as protector of my family. I was going to create a wholesome lifestyle void of television and modern conveniences, and embrace simple pleasures and clean living.

I promise I tried. I planted a garden; I started buying things like chickpea flour and organic produce. I made sure everything my baby touched was BPA-free and faithfully checked nutrition labels. I delayed two of my child's vaccinations because I trusted the ranting of former playboy bunny Jenny McCarthy over the advice of my doctor. I was going to be an earth mommy—with my baby secured in my organic cotton baby sling, wandering around the farmers market, making friends with the butcher, the baker and the candlestick maker.

It didn't take long for me to realize that our single-salary household couldn't bear the cost of this lifestyle. I enjoyed discussing choice cuts of beef and lamb with my friendly, blood-stained apron-wearing butcher, but soon realized his ground beef was a little steep at nine dollars a pound. My synthetic fertilizer-free garden failed to thrive, and I couldn't afford the near-100 percent price mark up for organic produce and to have trendy, organic milk delivered to my door (June Cleaver style). And while I flirted with the idea of switching to so-called "green" cleaners, I couldn't get past that sticky feeling left on my kitchen counters or sense that things just didn't feel as clean to me. Unclean surfaces and moldy-smelling bathrooms seemed a bigger threat to my kid than my lemony smelling regular (and less costly) spray cleaner.

It was a bit of a melancholy realization, but I knew that I simply didn't belong in this world populated with nervous mothers battling against the modern world. I also began to doubt what I was being told by all these so-called health and environmental advocates. Even to my untrained eye, much of the science cited seemed sloppy. I started doing more reading, more research, and was again filled with a new sense of purpose—and more than a little anger at those who prey on new moms like me and make our already hard jobs even harder.

Now, I'm committed to helping other mothers find their way out of this puffed up world of faux superiority and unnecessary worry that is the real product of too many media outlets geared toward scaring parents. I speak out against the radical activists that demonize harmless products and push government to needlessly meddle in our lives. I take a commonsense approach to scientific claims and attempt to translate those findings into normal, everyday life.

And that's why I'm writing this book. The truth is; I fell for it. I believed what they were telling me. Not anymore.

Here's who I am not: I'm not a scientist or a nutritionist; I'm not a doctor or a statistician. I'm a mother—a mother of three young, hungry, energetic boys—who is tired of those who try to make parenting, and plain old living, more complicated, stressful, and less fun than it should be.

Americans, particularly women, are bombarded with these alarmist messages about how the food they eat, the habits they practice, and the household products they use on a daily basis threaten their health and the health of their children. Parents are fed a trough of mixed messages: One study says a food item is dangerous while a competing study suggests the opposite. Women are warned that common items like shampoo, deodorant, plastic food containers, household disinfectants, children's toys, baby bottles, and garden hoses threaten them and their families. Alarmists have even cast living room furniture, hotdogs, trampolines, and open-toed shoes as a threat to children.

Yet the real damage comes after the alarmists have done their job of scaring the living daylights out of the general public. That's typically when the politicians and government regulators descend with promises to "save" us all from these dangers. They use these baseless fears to promote regulations that expand their power base.

The cost of this dynamic is high: wasted tax dollars, higher costs and inferior goods for consumers, fewer jobs in companies navigating through red tape. More importantly, we are all paying a personal cost with needless worry, and a less free, less happy society.

We deserve better.

This book starts with an overview of alarmism and how it works. I explain how activist organizations, the media, and government regulators work together to keep you worried in the hopes that you'll demand government action. I'll examine the effort to "nudge" you into better behavior and highlight some good news stories—the ones you rarely hear.

The second section examines how science and statistics become warped in the hands of the alarmists, and the third explores the "solutions" that alarmists push. They typically range from costly to harmful, and often are both. And worse, they discourage Americans from recognizing that they are responsible—not the government and not some corporation—for the health of their families, and that regular people are perfectly up to that job if they rely on common sense.

Next I highlight some of the ways we pay for alarmism, through higher prices, less variety, and fewer jobs. Yet while these are important, something just as important, but harder to put a price tag on, is the biggest casualty of alarmism: our freedoms and rich civil society. I don't know how to put a value on the loss when we discourage bake sales and lemonade stands, prevent kids from playing dodge ball at recess or having a drink from the garden hose, or tell moms that nearly everything they buy at the grocery store might harm their kids. But I do know that there is a cost, and it's a cost we shouldn't have to pay.

Finally, I provide you with some tools for how to fight back against alarmism, how to detect when some scare is trumped up, or if it's really reason for concern. It's critical that moms be able to discern between false alarmism and real risks.

I hope that after you read this book and take a look at the facts, you can take a deep breath, smile with a little more ease at your kids and your belongings, and then join me in fighting the alarmists.

PART I

....

THE MEDIA, ACTIVISTS, AND GOVERNMENT — HOW AND WHY THEY WANT YOU SCARED!

The bookshops are groaning under ziggurats of pessimism.
The airwaves are crammed with doom.
—Matt Ridley, *The Rational Optimist*

CHAPTER 1

THE CYCLE OF ALARMISM

I don't have to tell you things are bad.
Everybody knows things are bad.
—**Howard Beale**, *Network[2]*

. . . .

During dinner one evening, I was explaining to my husband (an IT security professional) that an environmental organization had just claimed children's raincoats contained "dangerous toxins." I half-jokingly suggested we should design a new line of "natural and chemical-free" children's rain gear. This new "smart, safe, and eco-friendly rain gear" would be made of humanely-slaughtered, oil-rubbed animal hides that had been stained with natural dyes like beet juice, cow urine and Gamboge tree resin. Terrified mothers—who had just cleaned out the coat closet—would be the company's first costumers.

We'd make a million bucks!

In response, my husband simply mumbled "FUD."

FUD? Prodding for more information, he explained the word was an acronym for "Fear, Uncertainty and Doubt," a marketing

3

term employed in the IT security field to sell products to nervous business executives. In his words, "there's no better way to sell a product than to say without it, your company will fail." He also explained that now more than ever FUD is used to influence the public and to promote government regulation—both in the IT sector and elsewhere.

For example, in 2009, Apple wanted to prevent users from hacking into their iPhones in order to download apps not approved by the company. Hoping to get regulators involved, Apple claimed that the nation's cellphone networks could suffer "potentially catastrophic" cyber-attacks if iPhone owners were permitted to tamper with their devices.

Terrifying, right?

Not really. Commenting to *Wired Magazine* about Apple's claim, one IT industry attorney said, "This kind of theoretical threat ... is more FUD than truth."[3] I'm sure even Apple executives chuckled as they came up with this action-movie-like claim. Yet the IT giant knew that if they managed to get the public sufficiently ginned up and convinced one or two legislators, they'd have a chance at pushing this regulation through.

The alarmist claims made by the food nannies, health, environmental, and anti-chemical activists, government regulators and power-hungry politicians are often equally outrageous. In fact, FUD is a common tool used against the public. It makes sense: By spreading fear, uncertainty and doubt, Americans will be alarmed and therefore more likely to acquiesce to whatever the alarmists want, whether that's paying more for a certain product or supporting more government regulations. If they freak out enough people, eventually someone is bound to say, "Something must be done." Those four words are music to a regulator's ears because those regulators are more than happy to swoop in and save the day with job-crushing and price-inflating regulations.

So, how exactly does the cycle of alarmism work? How do these groups use fear? How do they make consumers feel uncertain about their own personal decisions? How do they plant the seeds of doubt that products aren't safe?

Let's start with an example familiar to most moms: Bisphenol-A, more commonly known as BPA. While it is generally associated with baby products, BPA has been used since the early 1950s, most commonly as an epoxy sealant in canned food, which helps prevent bacterial contamination. BPA is also used to harden plastics for use in medical equipment, electronics, DVDs, car dashboards, eyeglass lenses, and plastic food containers. Yet, today, faux scientists with an anti-chemical ax to grind have declared BPA unsafe. This narrative has been allowed to fester and become part of popular culture despite hundreds of studies to the contrary. Today, BPA is blamed for everything from cancer to obesity, diabetes, heart disease, infertility and sexual problems.

Chemical alarmism was already quite ubiquitous when in 2011, an advocacy organization called the Breast Cancer Fund released a report claiming that, "There is a toxic chemical lurking in your child's Campbell's Disney Princess soup, in her Chef Boyardee pasta with meatballs, even in her organic Annie's cheesy ravioli."[4] The specific "toxic chemical" was BPA, which the report claimed "leaches into the food and is then consumed by adults and children alike."[5]

To illustrate that BPA had indeed leached into the food, the organization sent canned goods to a laboratory for analysis and, unremarkably, the results showed BPA was present in the food. Yet what the report left out was quite important: The amount of BPA in the food was far below what regulatory agencies consider safe.

So, what is safe? Well, according to the FDA's National Center for Toxicological Research (NCTR), which has been conducting in-depth studies of BPA since September 2008, there's not a whole lot to be worried about. From the FDA's website:

> The level of BPA from food that could be passed from pregnant mothers to the fetus is so low that it could not be measured. Researchers fed pregnant rodents 100 to 1,000 times more BPA than people are exposed to through food, and could not detect the active form of BPA in the fetus eight hours after the mother's exposure.
>
> Exposure to BPA in human infants is from 84 to 92 percent less than previously estimated.
>
> NCTR researchers report that they were able to build mathematical models of what happens to BPA once it's in the human body. These models showed that BPA is rapidly metabolized and eliminated through feces and urine. They found that BPA is "exactly the opposite" from some other toxins, like dioxin, that can stay in the body's tissues for months or even years.
>
> The center's toxicology research has not found evidence of BPA toxicity at low doses in rodent studies, including doses that are still above human exposure levels.[6]

The most recent study of BPA—which used human volunteers (I'll discuss the importance of human testing in chapter 4) who ate a diet high in BPA (they basically ate a lot of canned food)—showed that BPA is metabolized and excreted extremely rapidly.[7] Why is this important? Because it negates the very claim the alarmists make—that these chemicals (like BPA) "build up" in the body which is where the danger develops.

In other words, BPA simply doesn't hang around long enough to do any damage. Of course some trace amount of BPA may make its way into your bloodstream but that amount is so miniscule that it's hard to detect.

But alarmist groups are quick to change course if the science proves their claims wrong. Understanding that the jig was up on the "build up" narrative, alarmists simply began hand-wringing about a new danger, which lies in low-dose, rather than high-dose, exposure to BPA. The problem with this argument is that none of the experiments involving low doses of BPA have been replicated (a subject I'll also discuss later) and according to European Food Safety Authority, those studies "...were contradictory and not well conducted."[8]

Knowing that BPA quickly leaves the body is vitally important when considering alarmist reports—like the one produced by the Breast Cancer Fund. While I'm not going to argue with the organization's assertion that BPA leached into the canned food (it did!), the trace amounts are not high enough to make any sort of impact.

But, hey, you don't have to take my or the FDA's word for it. There are several other sources that come to the exact same conclusions. For instance, the EPA has certified that BPA is safe as used in food packaging. So did the European Union's Food Safety Authority, Japan's National Institute of Advanced Industrial Science and Technology, the Norwegian Scientific Committee for Food Safety. If you still don't believe me, how about asking the French (well-known to be scared of everything).

That's right, even the French Food Safety Agency thinks BPA is safe. Agreeing with the French are the Germans, the Canadians (While the Canadian government did ban BPA in baby products due to alarmist-engineered political pressure, the government has said BPA is safe.), the Australians and the New Zealanders.

Unfortunately for worried moms and dads, the actual science (as well as the various declarations of safety from international health organizations) meant little to the media and the blogging community. Soon after the Breast Cancer Fund released its paragon to junk science and without doing the most basic fact checking (or even a basic Google search), the media began churning out scary headlines:

"KIDS' SOUP CANS CONTAIN BPA TOXINS"[9]

"BPA IN CANNED FOODS: SHOULD YOU WORRY?"[10]

"YOUR KIDS ARE EATING THESE
CANNED FOODS LOADED WITH BPA" [11]

"BPA FOUND IN CANNED THANKSGIVING FOODS,
BREAST CANCER FUND REPORTS" [12]

Following this media blitz, mommy blogs lit up with warnings as parents nationwide began to worry that they were unknowingly poisoning their children. The already thriving BPA-free industry further capitalized on the alarmism while one company—which relied heavily on BPA to keep its canned food products safe—panicked. Campbell's Soup was already being pressured to remove BPA from the lining of its canned soups. Yet this didn't prepare them for the onslaught created by the Breast Cancer Fund report.

In fact, when one alarmist organization released a press statement saying that Campbell's planned to "phase out" the chemical,

Campbell's failed to issue even a basic correction. Soon the news spiraled out of control and the company had a new official position on the chemical: Campbell's would no longer use BPA.

But there was a major problem with this. Scientists haven't created an epoxy lining that works as well as BPA in protecting food from dangerous bacteria, which makes getting rid of the chemical rather tough. Science writer John Entine investigated this epic corporate communications failure in *Forbes*, writing:[13]

> "Wow. When we saw the headlines, we were just flabbergasted," my chemical executive friend told me. "We've been looking for alternatives for years. There's a large potential market for it. I didn't think the science was there yet. We just couldn't figure out how they did it."
>
> That's because Campbell's hasn't figured out how to do it either—and according to leading scientists inside the industry and out no breakthrough is in sight. Despite Campbell's public statements and hundreds of congratulatory media stories, the soup giant's basic manufacturing and research capabilities haven't progressed significantly in recent years. Like every canned goods company, it's very slowly edging away from using BPA in a tiny fraction of its low-acidic food lines. For the rest of its canned business—95% or more—Campbell's, like its competitors, will stick with what's safe and effective: BPA.[14]

Campbell's is in a tough situation. The company could correct the misinformation by explaining it has no intention of phasing out BPA, but then they will face alarmist accusations of turning a blind eye to their "killer" manufacturing methods (as characterized by the alarmists). Alternatively, the company could choose to use inferior sealants while investing even more research money, considerable company resources, and staff time to find a replacement product that works as well as BPA. That would put their customers at risk of bacteria, and another potential backlash.

Ultimately though, Campbell's should consider the far bigger issues at stake: Should companies roll over to the demands of radical activist groups—even when the demands are based on dubious scientific claims? Doesn't Campbell's have a duty to its customers to tell the truth about its manufacturing practices and the real safety issues at stake? Doesn't the company also have a duty to fight back against these activists who want to take perfectly good and safe products out of the marketplace?

Unfortunately, Campbell's has launched a rather milquetoast defense—one that tries (and fails) to straddle both camps—that of sound scientific evidence, which shows BPA to be completely safe, and that of the chemphobes who won't stop until BPA is no longer used in manufacturing. The company's conflict is obvious in a statement on its website which states: "We believe that current can packaging is one of the safest options in the world" but then adding that the company is "working to phase out the use of BPA in the lining of all of our canned products."[15]

Well, if companies are going to start operating under these guidelines, perhaps they should add "bullying" and "extortion" as a line item in their annual budgets. How about creating a budget line for "altering manufacturing methods to satisfy wacky alarmists?" Because if they refuse to fight back and set the record straight, these companies will pay and keep on paying.

One thing is clear from this example: Companies will respond to market and consumer demand—even if they've done nothing wrong. The entire Campbell's debacle should have demonstrated that government involvement isn't necessary because most corporations will go to ridiculous lengths to keep their customers happy.

Unfortunately, politicians didn't get the hint. Instead, based on the Breast Cancer Fund report (and many other alarmist claims), policy makers at every level of government around the country began proposing legislation to ban BPA. It became such a media and political storm that eventually, in 2012, the chemical industry formerly requested that the U.S. Food and Drug Administration (FDA) ban the use of BPA in baby products—a drastic yet effective strategy to prevent manufacturers from having to comply with hundreds of disparate and extremely complex state-level regulations. The *New York Times* reported on the FDA's move:

> Manufacturers have already stopped using the chemical in baby bottles and sippy cups, and the F.D.A. said that its decision was a response to a request by the American Chemistry Council, the chemical industry's main trade association, that rules allowing BPA in those products be phased out, in part to boost consumer confidence.[16]

This one act—the industry actually asking to be regulated—was a profound victory for the environmental, food and anti-chemical organizations that disseminate alarmism. It showed the alarmists that the scare-tactics they employ, the lies they tell, and the exaggerations they use, as well as their tendency to pass on incomplete information, is a successful strategy in scaring Americans into demanding unnecessary and expensive regulations on industry. The FDA's move to ban BPA sent a similarly strong, yet entirely inaccurate, message to consumers about BPA: It's dangerous! And the press has been more than willing to help promote this false image.

Yet ironically, in the FDA's most recent "official assessment" of BPA (issued March 2013), the agency actually confirmed *the exact opposite* about the chemical:

> FDA's current assessment is that BPA is safe at the very low levels that occur in some foods. This assessment is based on review by FDA scientists of hundreds of studies including the latest findings from new studies initiated by the agency.[17]

It's important to note that in this assessment, the FDA doesn't use clever language or even hint at the need for further research. The statement is clear: BPA is safe. The statement even goes further to say that the assessment was made after reviewing "hundreds of studies" that demonstrate the chemical's safety.

Unfortunately, the media isn't reporting the FDA's recent findings. In fact, an analysis of media reporting on BPA found 97 percent of stories on BPA framed the chemical as harmful and only two of the 87 stories that focused on the research surrounding BPA accurately reported that the FDA concluded that BPA is safe.[18]

It isn't just these multisyllabic chemicals that are being demonized by the alarmists. The foods and beverages Americans love to eat are also in the crosshairs. From sugary drinks and salty snacks to frozen vegetables and conventionally produced meat and dairy products, Americans are faced with increasingly scary stories about the food and beverages they consume.

The target of alarmists might change, but the narrative never does. When it comes to convincing the American public to back regulations on food and beverages, it's not enough to simply say, "Hey, that (insert high-calorie food here—Twinkie, Big Gulp, Whopper, milkshake) is gonna make you fat!" The alarmists know that they need to instill fear and make these food items seem dangerous and deadly.

In other words, employ FUD and sound the alarm!

Take Michael Jacobson, a well-known food nanny who coined the terms "junk food" and "empty calorie" and who helms the deeply feared alarmist organization The Center for Science in the Public Interest. He hates McDonalds ("McDonald's must stop exploiting children at some point"[19]), restaurant chains ("major restaurant chains are scientifically engineering these extreme meals with the express purpose of promoting obesity, diabetes, and heart disease"[20]), Fettuccini Alfredo ("heart attack on a plate"[21]), and fun ("Food dyes are added simply for their color to make foods fun. They serve no health purpose whatsoever"[22]).

When it comes to soda, Jacobson doesn't limit his advice to suggesting people might want to limit their consumption of full-sugar soda if they want to lose weight. No, no. That's not dramatic enough. Instead, Jacobson goes into full FUD mode, calling the beverage "a slow-acting but ruthlessly efficient bioweapon..."[23] Predictably, Jacobson adds, "The FDA should require the beverage industry to re-engineer their sugary products ... making them safer for people to consume, and less conducive to disease."[24]

Are these just the ramblings of a passionate food nanny?

Hardly. There's a method behind Jacobson's alarmism. In order to get the public sufficiently upset (and more critically, to get the public to demand a solution), Jacobson connects a particular behavior to a deadly disease. That's the best way to encourage the public to react.

The food nannies, like Jacobson, work hard to make this connection, but if you are paying attention, you'll see it's often a stretch: Most of the studies that they purport make this connection are observational studies that make correlations or associations, but fail to show direct causation between the food or beverages and the disease. That means that a study may claim to find that people who drink large quantities of soda are more likely than the average person to have heart disease, but it could just have easily made other correlations. For instance, the study's participants might also have reported a habit of eating pepperoni pizza, regularly consuming hearty farm-style breakfasts, and the majority of participants might also smoke and hate to exercise. These factors also impact a person's likelihood of developing health problems, but rather than report on all the study's findings, scientists will sometimes pick and choose the outcomes they're looking for.

It doesn't stop with the scientists conducting the research. In many cases, the environmental activists, food nannies, and politicians do the same when they use these types of studies to craft public policy. They select the correlation that best suits whatever "fix" they want to advance.

Food nannies have another tactic to spur action: Activists work to convince the American public that one individual's soda consumption impacts others. This clever rhetorical devise directs the obesity debate away from personal responsibility, proper nutrition and self-regulation toward a discussion of how obesity and obesity-related diseases will cost the government and taxpayers billions of dollars.

By framing the argument this way, your muffin top is no longer your private burden but rather a national budgetary concern and the legitimate purview of government officials.

Alarmists have it easy. They have a more than willing media to spread their scary stories. They have a nervous public who is increasingly told that common, everyday food and household items are a danger to them and their children. And they have power-hungry government officials who are eager to tap into new revenue sources or make themselves out to be the hero, saving moms and kids from harm.

This combustible combination means one thing for the average American: more fear, fewer facts, less money, and no fun. Oh yeah, and much less freedom.

CHAPTER 2

BE AFRAID...
OF EVERYTHING!

. . . .

Afew years ago, I was watching the news and was shocked to learn that my garden hose was incredibly dangerous. Say, what?

The newscaster anchoring the program that night seemed really upset about this story. He leaned forward in his seat, stuttered...and...wait...did I see him tear up? Did his voice just crack? Oh my gosh, he's going to cry!

This.is.a.serious.problem.

SOMETHING MUST BE DONE! NOW!

It's weird. I sometimes fall for it. I know I shouldn't but sometimes...only once in a while...I forget and fall into the alarmist trap. These news anchors seem so eager to protect me, so gallant, with such nice hair and skin. They look like they smell really good and take care of their teeth. They are genuinely concerned for my kids. I think they like me. I bet they'd want to hang out...

And then I snap out of it and remember that this is all part of the plan to freak me out so that I will welcome, even demand, the guiding hand of government. The alarmists and their media pals know that as a mom, I'm vulnerable to this type of messaging. They hope for this type of reaction: outrage, horror and fear.

Yet the real facts behind the "killer garden hoses lurking in your backyard" are hardly scary. The news story centered on the fact that most garden hoses are made of polyvinyl chloride, better known as PVC. PVC has high levels of lead and other chemicals and, therefore, the claim was that since children and pets sometimes drink from garden hoses, they were getting big doses of toxins when taking the occasional sip.

But before you read anymore, just think about it: Do children and pets really drink a lot of water from garden hoses? Is the garden hose a main source of water for children and pets? Are they drinking gallons of water this way?

Sure, during summer months, kids consume some "garden hose water" as they play in the sprinkler or splash in the kiddie pool. They may take a gulp or two when mom's watering the garden. But in general, kids do not get the bulk of their water in any given day—much less during their lives—from the garden hose. After all, the alarmists also tell us that kids drink too much juice and soda, and we know that doesn't come out of a garden hose.

I was lucky that I had time to look into this story and question its merits. I was able to ignore the hysteria, and consider the facts. And those facts are reassuring. Most garden hoses are indeed made of made of polyvinyl chloride, which is toxic if consumed in large quantities. Yet, it is impossible—let me repeat that word, *impossible*—for a human to consume enough water to reach toxic levels of PVC exposure. Why is this impossible? Because the amount of chemical that leaches into the water is so miniscule that a person would have to consume massive amounts of garden hose water in order for it to be a problem. And if a person attempted to drink the amount of water required to reach PVC toxicity, they'd first die of dilutional hyponatremia—death by water overdose—before reaching that toxic level.

In other words, you simply cannot poison yourself with garden hose water. You cannot harm yourself by the occasional sip of garden hose water. Again, it's impossible.

Alarmists naturally ignored this common sense and called for regulations on the garden hose industry. One terrified mommy blogger wrote: "I can't tell, looking at a hose, whether or not it is safe. Only a large scale overhaul of the regulations that govern what chemicals get into our stuff, such as the Safe Chemicals Act, can begin to protect us."[25] But so far manufacturers of garden hoses have been allowed to carry on with their businesses without having to jump through any new regulatory hoops.

But this doesn't mean there isn't a cost. Right now there are moms out there who are sitting on patios watching their toddlers run through the sprinkler or jump in the kiddie pool who are filled with fear of their garden hose. You can almost envision the scene: Instead of just enjoying the moment watching their kids play and laugh and work off some energy, these moms are periodically stopping to pester junior not to drink through the hose. The kids probably won't listen and will drink the water anyway, so then mom will become angry and begin yelling. Ultimately, she'll be left feeling defeated, worried, and scared. The kids will also feel bad, not enjoying the play as much and may even feel vaguely worried that they've endangered themselves. That may not impact the national economy, but it is making the country a worse place to live.

But these activist organizations don't seem to care that the anxiety level in this country is already off the charts. These groups understand that nervous parents are powerful allies in the effort to have manufacturers add warning labels to nearly every product they produce.

Yet, parents should also understand these warning labels come at a high cost to their bottom line because when the government mandates that a manufacturer alter its packaging or manufacturing practices, the costs associated with the changes aren't simply absorbed by the company. Rather, the costs are passed to consumers, most of whom never asked for these changes in the first place.

And while the alarmists like to say, unreservedly, that nearly everything sold in the grocery stores should come with a large warning label—on the front of the package—reasonable parents know these labels do next to nothing to protect children, especially as warning labels become so ubiquitous people inevitably tune them out.

Consider what is now being labeled a threat to our children. In 2010, the American Academy of Pediatrics (AAP) announced that "high-risk" foods like apples, chewing gum, chunks of peanut butter, hard candy, marshmallows, nuts, popcorn, raw carrots, sausages, seeds, grapes, and hot dogs should come with a warning label. The idea wasn't that there were nutritional problems with these items, but the AAP wanted parents warned that these foods posed a choking hazard to young children.[26]

But is choking as big a problem as the AAP portrays it to be?[27]

According to the Centers for Disease Control, 134 children under the age of four (that's the age range that children are most at risk for choking on food) died of suffocation in 2011. That's .0000556 percent of all children in this age range.[28] To put that rather hard to fathom fraction in perspective: Your child is four times more likely to be struck by lightning (.0002 percent) than choke on his food. And not all of those asphyxiation deaths were caused by food. In fact, according to the CDC data, only 25 percent were caused by food being lodged in the airway. The other 75 percent of deaths were the result of accidental hangings, choking on non-food items, suffocating on bed sheets or unspecified problems with breathing. While the death of any child is tragic, we need some perspective: Choking deaths among children are rare, and choking deaths caused by food are even more rare.

Yet, this reassuring data hasn't stopped the AAP demanding food manufactures add warning labels and "redesign" certain food items, such as hot dogs, so the size, shape and texture make them less likely to lodge in a child's throat. Janet Riley, president of the National Hot Dog and Sausage Council (uh, yes, this organization actually exists), injected a little bit of common sense into the great "hot dog reshape" debate saying:

> As a mother who has fed toddlers cylindrical foods like grapes, bananas, hot dogs and carrots, I 'redesigned' them in my kitchen by cutting them with a paring knife until my children were old enough to manage on their own.[29]

But relying on a parent's common sense simply isn't good enough for alarmists like Dr. Gary Smith, the lead author of the AAP statement, who said in a *USA Today* article that "No parents can watch all of their kids 100% of the time...The best way to protect kids is to design these risks out of existence."[30]

He's correct. Parents simply cannot be expected to watch children 100 percent of the time, and this does indeed leave children vulnerable to dangers. Yet, Smith's simplistic solution to "design risks out of existence" is unrealistic and incredibly naive. How will we rid the world of stones? Coins? Marbles? The keys off of the computer keyboard that my industrious two-year-old once pried out to pop in his mouth? Does Dr. Smith suggest we place children in a bubble to keep them safe from every possible environmental danger?

After all, young children face far greater risks than choking. In fact, a far greater cause of injuries among children (0-14) is falling down—a pretty common occurrence among humans learning to walk and run. The CDC estimates that about 2.8 million children go to the emergency rooms each year because they fall down and hurt themselves.[31] In Dr. Smith's super safe world stairwells would be banned, high surfaces made illegal and common items in a home—like tables and bookshelves—gathered up and destroyed. What else Dr. Smith would like to see "designed out of existence?"

A better solution might be for the AAP to advise parents to look at a food and determine for themselves its choking potential. Perhaps the AAP could remind parents to tell their kids to eat slowly, take smaller bites and chew. Unfortunately, personal responsibility isn't enough for your benevolent government minder who thinks you're an idiot.

Again, common sense isn't the only casualty here. Dr. Smith and his colleagues at the AAP seem not to understand this, but industry will need to spend money—money that could go to job creation, bonuses for employees, or the creation of other, perhaps healthier, products—on redesigning foods to suit their nanny predilections.

Of course, we all want to reduce risks for our children. Yet life itself comes with a certain amount of risk and it's the job of competent adults to mitigate life's risks and to teach children to do the same. Learning how to handle life's risks is critical to human development, and it would be a problem if parents failed to teach children how to assess risks on their own.

After all, there's no need to advise your child to chew food completely before swallowing if all food is redesigned to prevent choking. You don't need to tell your kid to stop climbing on high spaces if there are no high spaces to climb. If we do away with cars, there's no need to tell the kids to look both ways when you cross the road... and on and on. Reasonable people understand that eliminating all risk during childhood isn't possible, and wouldn't even be desirable if it was possible.

Parents want information so that they can make good decisions for themselves and their families. They should reject those who encourage them to worry about everything under the sun (speaking of that scary, dangerous sun...). It's not healthy for them, and it's not healthy for children.

Occasionally, parents should even sit back and appreciate how we are all extremely fortunate to be raising our kids in the modern era where common diseases have been eradicated, child death is rare and modern conveniences make our lives not just easier, but a lot more fun. We should protect our children from true dangers, but not get so overwhelmed that we forget to enjoy life. In fact, I would say the destructive, alarmist culture is one aspect of the modern world that you really should try to keep away from your family.

CHAPTER 3

YOUR LESSER ANGELS
WILL ALWAYS WIN

*E*ach day, I tell my children what to do and how best to behave. I explain what's good for them and what to avoid in the hopes that someday they'll be able to make their own good and healthy decisions. I direct their interactions with other people, demanding they be polite, kind and communicate clearly. Sometimes I have to yell at them to stay away from the street and to stop fighting. I expect them to be good when I need to run errands and punish them if they act out. I decide what they eat and make all of their meals. I don't suffer picky eaters or indecision.

Let's face it, being ordered around and yelled at is the down side of being a kid. But, it isn't all bad. My kids get to sleep in (I pray they do on the weekend). They get to jump in the sprinkler half-naked and no one notices. Kids get to take naps, eat cupcakes and doughnuts without guilt, play dress-up and climb trees. My kids

25

have no responsibilities beyond "wash your hands!" and "put your dishes in the sink." Heck, for a few years, kids don't even have to make it to the bathroom in time.

Yet, in general, kids don't have the freedom to decide how they live. If my kids had that sort of freedom, they'd be living in the trees, inviting stray dogs, cats and frogs to stay the night, and living on a diet of lollipops and gummy bears.

That's why parents are important. The ordering around, the yelling, the expectations and constant directing and correcting are all done for a reason. Parents help their kids grow up to make good decisions. We want to see our children exhibit good judgment and an understanding of consequences. They should need us less and less as they grown up.

This is the natural, linear development of children into adulthood, and it's worked for generations to produce responsible citizens. Yet, more and more now, we don't expect good judgment and maturity from adults. In fact, increasingly, adults are being infantilized by government officials who have a rather depressing opinion of the human race. In short, they don't think people are capable of making good decision for themselves.

Enter New York City Mayor Michael Bloomberg who in 2011 announced plans to institute a size restriction on sugary beverages sold in the city. The rule was complicated. It limited consumers to 16-ounce cups if the drink contained more than 25 calories per eight ounces. Yet, the ban was not comprehensive. For instance, the ban did not apply to fruit juices or fruit smoothies, which often contain more calories than soda. It also didn't apply to alcoholic beverages: good news for beer lovers and for those 600+ calorie margarita drinkers. Milkshakes were also excluded from the ban, which meant New Yorkers could indulge if they craved a 24-ounce, 2,000-calorie

Cold Stone Creamery peanut butter and cookie milk shake—which incidentally was named by *Men's Health Magazine* as the worst drink on its list of 20 Worst Drinks in America.[32] The magazine said of the shake:

> In terms of saturated fat, drinking this Cold Stone catastrophe is like slurping up 68 strips of bacon. Health experts recommend capping your saturated fat intake at about 20 grams per day, yet this beverage packs more than three times that into a cup the size of a Chipotle burrito. But here's what's worse: No regular shake at Cold Stone, no matter what the size, has fewer than 1,000 calories. [33]

Yup, no ban on these confections!

The ban was also unevenly applied based on where beverages were sold. For instance, the ban applied to restaurants while convenience stores—where one can purchase those iconic Big Gulps—weren't covered. These inconsistencies didn't stop Bloomberg from proceeding.

Citing rising obesity rates (despite the fact that obesity rates were declining in the city at the time the Mayor announced the ban), the Mayor defended the ban saying "we're not taking away anybody's right to do things, we're simply forcing you to understand that you have to make the conscious decision to go from one cup to another cup."[34]

Forcing you? Normally, politicians avoid the word "force." Yet, Bloomberg sees policies like soda restrictions, gun control, smoking and trans-fat bans as an acceptable use of force. You know, because it makes people do things that are good for them.

Bloomberg sees things very clearly: Government is good and can be trusted; individuals are weak-willed and dim-witted (never mind that the government is made up of equally weak-willed and dim-witted people). That means the government has to oversee the common man and take a bigger role in his life to protect him. In fact, soon after Bloomberg's soda ban was struck down by a New York City judge (for being capricious and difficult to enforce), Bloomberg actually told NBC News "I do think there are certain times we should infringe on your freedom."[35]

Bloomberg's policies are the manifestation of Nudge Theory—a concept in the field of behavioral science, which holds that people can be "encouraged" to make the decisions of which government approves. The theory, which gained popularity after the 2008 publication of a book on the subject by economist Richard Thaler and former Obama administration regulation czar Cass Sunstein, suggests that instead of forcing certain behaviors (using that messy totalitarian-re-education-camp-do-it-or-I'll-shoot-you-in-the-head approach), governments can give people the impression that they've made their own decisions all the while manipulating people's "choice environments."

The term "choice environments" might sound technical and wonky, but really it's no different than how I treat my young children. I like to give my children that whiff of choice while at the same time limiting their options to the items I choose. For example, on any given day, you might hear me say: "Hey boys, I'll let you decide; carrots or apples for lunch today. Which one?"

Isn't that nice? I've given my children the impression that they made a choice when in reality I was in charge all along. I do this because I want them to learn to make decisions, but also because they are children and I want to control the outcomes because I do know better than they do.

Nudge theorists have the same view of adults. They believe choices must be tightly controlled, because people are simply incapable of making good and healthy decisions. As Cass Sunstein explained in a recent article on obesity: "Our eating is mindless or automatic in that we tend to eat whatever is in front of us," and that, like zombies, people "eat whatever is put in front of them, even if they aren't hungry."[36]

Nudge theory makes sense if you share Sunstein's rather dismal view of the average American: lazy, simple-minded, voraciously hungry, and incapable of controlling themselves or having any sort of concern for their own health. Like children, these people must be trained, guided, monitored and ultimately controlled.

This isn't just the opinion of gloomy behavioral scientists. This is an opinion held by most food nannies and alarmists. Food writer and nutritionist Marion Nestle is convinced you have trouble controlling yourself. Speaking to National Public Radio about government's role in people's eating habits, Nestle said "People don't really have a lot of control over what they eat. I know that sounds completely ridiculous, but if you give somebody a large portion of food, or if you put food in front of someone, that person is going to eat it."[37]

If Nestle—who is considered a respected author and nutritionist—really believes this, what does she make of the $20 billion weight-loss industry, which includes diet books, diet drugs and weight-loss surgeries. How about the 108 million people currently dieting in the United States?[38] Clearly someone in America is working hard to gain control over his or her weight and food decisions.

Of course, Nestle's low opinion of the average American is well-known. Discussing the nutrition labels that are required by law to be printed on all packaged food, Nestle suggested the simple addition, subtraction and division required to read these labels is too taxing and that people will have trouble figuring out the per-serving amount of calories printed on the label. She suggested people should be free from this difficult task, saying, "I don't think people should have to do the math."[39] One suspects Nestle doesn't think the average American can actually do the math. Nestle also objects to where the labels are placed on the food product, demading food manufacturers put the nutrition information on the front of the package. Why the change? Apparently, in addition to being mathmatically challenged, you're too dumb to turn the package over to view the nutrition information already located on the back of the box.

New York Times food columnist Mark Bittman and food writer Michael Pollan share Nestle's concerns about average folks figuring out how to eat. Both suggest the food industry makes it difficult for eaters to make good decisions. Food activist and lawyer Michelle Simon told the website Nourishlife.org that Americans need to get over the idea that food is a personal choice.

I believe that its offensive for government, and these various food nannies, to presume to know better than citizens and attempt to herd us all toward better health. Even if government bans and regulations were effective, I'd still be uncomfortable with this idea since I simply don't believe that it's government's role to intervene in the personal lives of (supposedly) free people.

Yet there is little to suggest this government meddling even works. According to a study published last year in the *American Journal of Clinical Nutrition*, instead of helping people make healthier decisions, limiting people's high-calorie food options does nothing to reduce their overall calorie intake or help them lose weight. [40] The result suggests the far better approach is to expand consumer choices instead of limiting them.

Luckily, for millions of dieters, that's precisely what's happening today.

According to a new study from The Hudson Institute and the Robert Wood Johnson Foundation, between 2006 and 2011, lower-calorie foods and beverages were the key growth engine for restaurants.[41] The study showed that there was a 5.5 percent increase in sales among chains selling lower-calorie meals compared to a 5.5 percent decline in other chains. Another telling finding in the study was that sales of french fries are declining in both number of servings and share of total food servings among fast food chains, and people are choosing low-calorie beverages over traditional beverages.

Women—the primary grocery shopper in most American households—don't need some fancy research paper to tell them these obvious truths. They know it because they are the ones walking down the snack food aisle where they can see the various options provided to consumers: low salt, no salt, low fat, no fat, reduced calorie, multigrain, organic, high fiber, dairy free, gluten free, vegan, etc. Ultimately, more choices make it easier for people to make healthier decisions and to tailor their diets to their specific health needs.

These choices are also helping Americans live healthier and longer than at any time in history. In fact, counter to the alarmists' doom and gloom messages, there is a lot of good news out there to share. Here are just a few helpful data points if you ever find yourself in a group of Debbie Downer alarmists (of course, we hope this never happens to you!):

+ There are more 90-year-olds in this country than ever be-fore. In fact, the number of near-centurions has almost tri-pled since 1980, to 1.9 million. [42]

+ According to the National Cancer Institute, cancer rates have declined among men since 1975 and declined for wom-en until 2006 (at which point rates stabilized).[43]

+ According to the CDC, death rates for all race and ethnic groups have been decreasing since 1950 which can be at-tributed to ongoing reductions in death rates from heart disease, cancer, stroke, and chronic lower respiratory dis-eases.[44]

+ Children born today can expect to live longer than ever in U.S. history.[45]

+ According to "The State of US Health, 1990 – 2010," pub-lished in 2013 in the *Journal of the American Medical Asso-ciation*, since 1990, many common childhood diseases have become less prevalent.[46]

+ According to a new Harvard study based on data collected over almost 20 years on nearly 90,000 individuals, even as life expectancy increases, with the exception of the year or two just before death, people are healthier than they used to be.[47] In other words, people are adding healthy years, not debilitated years, to their lifespans.

Today, living a long life isn't just a matter of chance. Increasingly now, it is a choice we make. Sure, some people will meet an early death due to unforeseen accidents, war, criminal acts, and infec-tious diseases, but overall humans are living longer and dying of old age. We can reduce the likelihood of contracting those diseas-es that continue to plague our society by living a healthy life. But ultimately, being healthy and "living clean" is a choice one has to make—a choice one must be free to make.

It certainly isn't pleasant to think about people deliberately making choices that will shorten their lifespans. But that's part of living in a free society. People need to be free not only to make good and healthy decisions, but to make bad decisions as well. And we should be careful about assuming that what's a bad decision for one person is a bad decision for everyone.

That's a fact food alarmists miss as they hand wring about people's personal food decisions: Some "bad" decisions are linked to fun and happiness. And being happy and having a good 'ole time is also good for your health. The food alarmists might not understand why someone would choose to order a burger and fries, but plenty of burger fans understand: It tastes good. It makes people happy.

Sadly, the alarmists often seem to overlook the value of happiness. They miss that totalitarian-like attempts to control others' personal decisions are a bit of mood killer. They may claim that they are working to make us all healthier and put us on the road to a longer life, but they fail to understand that they can make life—long or short—miserable. And that's not good for anyone.

PART II

....

THE MISUSE
OF SCIENCE

Extraordinary claims require extraordinary evidence
—Carl Sagan[48]

CHAPTER 4

MOM'S GUIDE
TO GOOD SCIENCE

87% OF WOMEN REPORT HAVING A TOUGH TIME FINDING SOURCES ABOUT HEALTH AND SAFETY THEY CAN TRUST

- IWF POLL

IWF.ORG   ALARMISM

osting a play-date one afternoon, I offered my children and the visiting child a simple snack of sliced apples, whole grain pretzel rods, and ice cold milk. Assuming the child's mother would approve of the healthy snack, I didn't think I needed to ask if her son could join in. Yet, as I placed the apple slices on my children's favorite Avengers plastic plates, the mother meekly inquired if the apples were organic.

"Nope," I proudly responded.

She told me her child would pass on the apples.

As I was pouring the milk, she asked even more sheepishly, "Is that organic milk?"

"Heck no! Look around, we're not millionaires," I shot back with a laugh.

I was trying to keep it light, but this mom was dead serious and not at all in the mood to joke around about the food I was offering her child. She told me her child would just drink the bottled water she'd brought from home. I thought that was the end of it, but as we sat the children down at the kitchen table with their separate snacks and beverages, the mother seemed genuinely concerned for my children.

"Did you know that those non-organic apples are on the 'dirty dozen' list?" she nervously asked, referring to a list compiled by a radical environmental group that ranks the fruits and vegetables with the highest levels of pesticide residue (residue, by the way, that is at very low-levels and the Environmental Protection Agency considers safe).

"They're just coated in pesticides," she warned, adding "the latest studies say pesticides cause cancer and all sorts of problems for children."

I tried to explain to this mom that the "dirty dozen" list was nothing more than alarmist twaddle. I described how the EPA monitors the fruits and vegetables sold in grocery stores to ensure residue levels remain below what the EPA considers safe.

I tried to use a visual, telling her that her son would have to eat hundreds of apples and still would likely fall below the level regulators have deemed safe.[49] But I could see her eyes glaze over with each calming word I uttered. Instead of pressing the point further, I just changed the subject. I didn't want to fight. After all, we were having a play-date, not a college debate, and I wanted to have a pleasant afternoon.

Truthfully, I had sympathy for this mom. She was nervous, and her mind was made up. No amount of encouragement from me was going to make her feel better about my dirty apples. But it did teach me a lesson. It demonstrated the power these organizations have over parents—particularly women who purchase most of the food for the family.

The fear I saw in this women's face was the product of two very combustible phenomena that are attributes of our era: 1) the culture of alarmism and 2) the rise in "helicopter parents"—parents so concerned about their children's welfare that they hover, like helicopters, above their children, attending to their every need and watching out for any conceivable danger. Helicopter parents are big consumers of alarmist information. In fact, they thrive on alarmism, believe it wholeheartedly, and eagerly pass it on to other nervous parents as a sort of public service. Which brings us to the third category of parent—the confused and frightened parents who can't afford to buy the high-end, boutique products but who live with the guilt and constant fear of not knowing what to believe and being worried they're hurting their children. These are the parents I'm most concerned about and to whom this book is dedicated.

Helicopter parents also act on the information—with their money. With each claim of danger (it doesn't matter if it's legitimate or junk science), these parents change their purchasing habits. They might begin purchasing specialty and much more expensive clothing (all cotton, no dyes please!), food (organic, sustainable, no preservatives or artificial coloring, no GMOs, cage- and cruelty-free, of course, humanely slaughtered, whole grain, salt and sugar free, etc.), toys (chemical-free and brain challenging for our little genius), furniture (no flame-retardants and only those pieces that use wood from "thoughtfully managed forests,"[50] please!), household cleaners (eco-friendly for us!), and personal care products (paraben-, formaldehyde- and cruelty-free, of course!).

When you compare these parents with someone like me, the differences are clear. Unlike my nervous friend and her fellow helicopter parents, I'm not worried about the nonorganic apples my children eat. Nor did I give a second thought to the conventionally-produced milk I pour into their sippy cups at each mealtime. I don't care that the pretzel sticks I buy are the store brand, not some trendy brand that costs twice as much and promises to be all-natural and without added this and that. I'm happy I'm able to save money on these cheaper products and give my kids get a healthy snack to boot.

So, how do you get such disparity? How can one mom (my friend) be so nervous about nearly everything with which her child comes in contact while the other (me) yawns at the many warnings issued to mothers every day? Why do I feel confident and unafraid? How can I so easily ignore the ubiquitous alarmist claims that appear daily in the media about everything from playground equipment to raincoats?

It's simple. I've learned to tell the difference between legitimate science and dangers, and the nonsense peddled by the alarmists. I know the hallmarks of a good scientific study and genuine research. I understand that the alarmists know that two little words—"studies say"—give their claims that whiff of legitimacy that will sway people, and that "study" has become such a broad and abused term that it really means very little.

Having the ability to differentiate between solid science and junk science is critical if you are going to navigate through the culture of alarmism.

Here are some of the questions you should ask when trying to determine if a study is legit or junk:

Question #1: Who is behind the study?

It is critically important to consider the source of a study. Because organizations (on each side of the debate) want to cite statistics or research studies that bolster their goals, these groups will go to great lengths to produce data that does just that. After all, if these groups want to keep the lights on and continue to pay their employees, they need to keep their worried and dues-paying followers as nervous as possible. In other words, alarmism = donations.

Sometimes alarmist organizations seem frustrated that the scientific community isn't providing frightening-enough studies. To remedy this, these groups simply release in-house "studies," "reports," or "investigations" designed and formatted to look like official scientific research studies. Naturally, these in-house publications claim to reveal new and groundbreaking information (usually a newly discovered connection between a certain food, chemical, or behavior with a terrible, crippling disease). Yet, when one really analyzes the material, it becomes clear that these publications are nothing more than alarmist nonsense dressed up to look scientific.

It's also important to consider the "news" source promoting the study. Certain organizations present themselves as news outlets, but they're really nothing more than media engines dedicated to cranking out scary stories. Two such organizations are NaturalNews.com and Mercola.com. These two organizations are well-known as procurers of alarmist and inaccurate information. While these websites sometimes publish helpful articles ("Probiotics help reduce stress"), they also promote studies long after the wider scientific community has debunked them.

So, watch out for studies (and "news" stories about these studies) that come from groups with an ax to grind. There's a good chance they've fudged the results.

Question #2: How big is the study?

Many studies examine the habits and behaviors of people—how much soda they drink; how much time they spend exercising; how much sleep they get at night. This information is gathered, comparisons are made, and relationships are detected from the data. In general, for these comparisons to provide useful guidance and information, it's important that they include a large sample size. This isn't to say all small studies are bad, but, in general, a bigger sample yields more reliable results.

For a non-scientific visualization of this concept, think of the world as a giant pie—a pie so big, one person can't possibly eat it all. So, to figure out if the pie tastes good, a slice is cut out. Of course, the taster doesn't know if this slice is an accurate representation of the whole pie. Maybe the slice cut has more berries in it, or maybe the crust was thicker on that side of the pie, or maybe one side of the pie is slightly undercooked while the other is cooked just right. These things cannot be controlled, yet because the pie is so big, only a small part of it can be tasted. The solution, therefore, is to slice as big a piece of the pie as possible, or even better take several slices from different parts of the pie. That way, you get a bigger representation of the whole pie, which will reduce the likelihood that what you taste is different from the whole. Scientists operate on the same principle. Larger sample sizes create less doubt of the study's results.

It's also important that we know how the researchers selected their sample. Were participants picked at random among all ages, and races? Or was everyone in the study a twenty-three year old living in an urban area with a history of substance abuse? If the later, the results may be very important for people with similar characteristics, but not for my husband, parents and me.

Unfortunately, alarmists don't always tell you when they've used a small or homogenous sample. They sometimes fail to explain that the findings apply only to a very small subset of the population. In fact, it's common for alarmist groups to use the results of very small studies (some involving less than 20 participants) to generate big, scary headlines.

So, remember, small studies can be interesting, but more often than not, the headlines they generate belong in the junk pile.

QUESTION #3: WHAT WAS THE TIMEFRAME FOR THE STUDY, THE SUBJECTS AND THE DOSE?

It's also important to consider the length of a study when considering the impact of certain things on the human body. For instance, if a study claims a certain product is harmful, it's important to follow study participants for a certain number of years to ascertain the long-term impact. Good studies take time. So, watch out for studies that observe participants over a short timeframe.

Similarly, people should consider the exposure levels to a given product and ask how much relevance it has to the real world. If a rat is injected with nail polish every day, is it really a surprise that the rat will develop health problems? This doesn't really tell me much, however, about any health impact of me painting my nails once a month.

FDA scientists Ronald J. Lorentzen and David G. Hattan recently wrote about the tendency of activist organizations to ignore the important issue of "dose" in order to drive home their scientifically inaccurate point and overstate risks. In the online journal *Nature*, the scientists explained, "[V]irtually every situation or substance is hazardous under some conditions, or at some dose, and to refer to hazard (detection) alone paints a profoundly deficient portrait of risk to the public."[51]

In other words, even your sweet grandmother's homemade rice pudding will kill you...if you eat two tons of it.

QUESTION #4: DID PARTICIPANTS SELF-REPORT?

At a dinner party years ago, one of the guests—a family physician—told me that when his patients answer the question "how much do you drink per week?" he always multiplies the answer they give ("oh... you know...two or three glasses") by six. The reason for this multiplication: Most people lie. That's true for studies that rely on self-reported data as well.

In general, people want to be good and demonstrate that they make healthy decisions. It makes sense then that even when people are filling out a survey—even when the results will be anonymous—people tend to fudge the answers; some just a little, some a lot!

The point: A study that relies on data that has been self-reported doesn't always provide the most reliable information. It may tell us about how people feel about issues, how they wish they would behave or think they ought to, but they often tell us very little about what is really going on.

QUESTION #5: IS THE WORD "CORRELATION" OR "ASSOCIATION" USED IN THE FINDINGS?

Studies that claim to have found a correlation or an association don't automatically belong in the junk pile, but it's important to understand the limits of these studies. The primary problem is that correlations are pretty easy to find.

For instance, a study published in October 2011 in the journal *Injury Prevention* suggested that soda consumption leads to violence in children.[52] The study found that teens who consumed five cans of full sugar soda or more each week were 9 to 15 percent more likely than non-soda drinkers to be violent toward others or to engage in aggressive activities, such as carrying a gun or knife to school.[53]

Naturally, the study grabbed headlines—most of which blamed soda consumption for teen violence. This narrative was helpful to those working to regulate the beverage industry, but not to those who are actually concerned about reducing teen violence. That's because the researchers cherry picked the results and encouraged the understanding that there was a causal relationship—soda-drinking leads to violence—when there is no reason to assume a relationship exists at all.

Let's use a little common sense when looking at this issue. Kids drinking large quantities of sugary soda each week are probably able to do so because their parents aren't around to monitor that child's eating habits and to encourage healthy behaviors. If parents aren't around to see little Johnny drinking three gallons of soda every day, it's a good guess that they don't know a lot about Johnny's friends or if Johnny has begun engaging in bad or violent behavior. It therefore makes sense that another factor at work here (i.e. parenting) is more likely to be driving both the high consumption of soda and the violent behaviors.

Here are just a few of the other correlations that might have been found, and the corresponding headlines:

✦ "Bad Parenting Causes Violent Children"
✦ "Failure to Teach Kids Basic Manners Results in Soda-Swigging Thuggery"
✦ "Violent Teens Show Flagrant Disregard for Proper Nutrition"

The bottom line: Correlations are easy to find and cherry pick. Actual causation is much more difficult to find and has much more relevance.

QUESTION #6: DID THE STUDY INVOLVE RATS?

Scientists are limited. Ethics prevents them from testing their theories on humans. Instead, they often use rats. Two things to know about lab rats: 1) rats have a short life span; 2) rats are prone to developing tumors.

With this in mind, consider a 2011 report on BPA in canned food released by a well-known alarmist public health organization called the Breast Cancer Fund. The report said that eating canned foods "beyond a single serving on a regular basis could lead to exposure to levels of BPA that have been associated with abnormalities in breast development and increased risk of developing breast cancer, and adverse effects on brain development, reproductive development, prostate weight, testis weight, puberty onset, body weight, metabolic immune system functions, and gender-related behaviors including aggression and some social behaviors."[54]

Boy, that sounds really scary! And you should be scared...if you're a rat residing in a cage in a laboratory. That's because the "studies" cited in the Breast Cancer Fund's report all involved rats injected with extremely high doses of BPA—doses much higher than anyone would ever receive by eating a few servings of Campbell's chicken noodle soup.

In fact, of the seven studies cited, only one was conducted on humans, and that one study involved women who were already at high risk of developing cancer. In this study, the researchers actually "introduced" the donor's "high-risk . . . breast epithelial cells to BPA in concentrations that are detectable in human blood, placenta and milk."[55] In other words, the cells were directly injected with a massive dose of BPA. Luckily for us, the canned food industry isn't lurking around corners to stab innocent chicken-noodle-soup-loving women and children in the arm with a syringe full of BPA.

What the Breast Cancer Fund failed to discuss in their report was another study released the same year by a team of scientists from U.S. Food and Drug Administration (FDA), the Centers for Disease Control and Prevention (CDC), and the Pacific Northwest National Laboratory. That study involved not rats, but humans who volunteered to eat a diet with higher levels of BPA than is normally consumed by the average American. Their blood and urine was then collected and analyzed and the results showed that in the majority of samples, no BPA was detected.

The bottom line: If a study involves rats, it doesn't always indicate human reaction will be the same.

QUESTION #7: WHAT IS THE "SCIENTIFIC CONSENSUS" ON THIS ISSUE?

Science is frustrating. It's fluid and fickle. It's capricious and dynamic. Scientific research doesn't operate like a treasure hunt with scientists running around in their white lab coats, treasure map in hand, trying to locate that elusive chest of gold and then grabbing it for keeps. Instead, science is a process of slow discovery. Scientists posit a question, test it by doing experiments, analyze the data collected, and finally draw some sort of conclusions. This process is called the scientific method, and for thousands of years, scientists have used it to discover more about the world in which we live.

But scientists don't just pack up and go home after this process is complete. There's more work to be done. In fact, this is where the really important work begins. The first step is checking one's work. In studies that are particularly large, produce surprising results, or focus on important health-related topics, the scientist repeats the experiment to test if he can get the same results.

In non-wonky terms (and to continue with our pie analogy...can you tell I like pie?), imagine one of those pie-baking contests at the county fair. Participants train like Olympians to make their recipe come out the same each time. Contestants practice for months beforehand to make sure that the piecrust is as flaky and tender as possible. They measure and weigh the ingredients carefully to ensure that on the big day—the day when their pie goes before the board of judges—they have recreated their famous, award winning, blue ribbon recipe. For these cooks, replication is critical if they're going to get the same dish each time. Scientists working in a lab are really no different. If a study is going to be taken seriously, the scientist must ensure that the results can be replicated.

But science isn't a solitary field. In fact, good science depends on regular interactions within the scientific community—this is known as the peer review process, which serves as a check on scientists' work.

The first step in the peer review process is for the scientist to communicate his findings at a professional conference or through some other medium so that other experts can learn about this latest research. The scientist must release the full details of his study and the experiments he's performed (this is why reputable studies always have a section called "methods" so that other scientists can evaluate and repeat the study).

Inviting others to evaluate and repeat the experiments is a process called "replication" and, just like the scientists that first ran the experiment, it means running the same experiment over and over to ensure the results can be reproduced (but this time by any scientist and in any lab). If the results can't be replicated, the experiment probably wasn't done well in the first place or perhaps the results were skewed because of contamination or some unseen influence on the variables. Replication also helps detect accidental error as well as fraud.

After all of this is done, the study is published and then subject to even more scrutiny, criticism, or, if warranted, praise. Based on the now-published study, other scientists will build on what was learned. Other studies will be conducted. After years of studying a particular subject, "scientific consensus" may be reached.

Of course, reaching scientific consensus doesn't indicate the science is settled. Science is never settled. Rather, it indicates a sort of agreement among colleagues that the issue has been thoroughly studied and that scientists sorta, kinda, know what in the heck is going on.

Scientific consensus does not mean unanimity. There will always be outliers—studies that come to different conclusions. Yet, more often than not, the studies outside the consensus usually fail to pass the smell test. They cannot be replicated; the study's authors fail to divulge the methodology, or there is a flaw in the study design. While one doesn't have to totally dismiss the scientific studies that lie outside of consensus, it's critical that those interested in these subjects understand where they belong in the bigger picture. As science writer Fourat Janabi writes, it's important to put them in their proper place:

> Think of it this way: the scientific literature of a particular field is an engine, full of gears and cogs; most of them spin forward, though a few spin backwards. So, if you want the whole picture, you must look at the engine (the literature and the consensus is the mechanic), not at a single study, to properly absorb and hopefully understand, the field; for while most gears spin forward, some spin backwards.[56]

The complexity of scientific research makes it easy to misunderstand and easy for alarmists to misuse.

I often think of that mom from my play-date when I read the latest alarmist claims. I imagine her cleaning out her pantry and the medicine cabinets (for the eighth time that year). I can see her furiously scratching things off her grocery list after reading of a new food scare or about some multi-syllabic word she doesn't understand. I wonder if she ever follows up on these issues, to read the calm analysis of these scary studies, which usually says there's not much to worry about. I wonder if she ever stops worrying. Probably not.

You don't have to be that mom. You can keep your eyes out for the latest news about the health information that might impact your family, but do it in a smart way. Look past the headlines. See what was really studied and by whom. Is it really something that you have to be on the look out for, or is it one with little relevance to your situation?

Many times, you'll find that most of the risks being hyped by the media are really very small. I'm sure you'll find some that give you pause and might encourage you to make a little change in what you are doing, but mostly you'll see that common sense and moderation in all things—and that includes worry—is usually the best course.

CHAPTER 5

STUDIES SAY...

*We live in a virtual junkyard of information,
a growing, steaming pile of statistical garbage
and toxic nonsense that won't decay and disappear.*
—**Trevor Butterworth**, *Forbes*[57]

. . . .

*L*ast year, my son returned home from his first day of kinder-
garten with an inch-thick stack of papers I was required to review. The stack included a few field trip permission slips, a parent
volunteer form or two, the PTA meeting schedule, the after-school
program information, and other tips on how to get through the year.

It all seemed like pretty standard stuff until I came across a col-
orful pamphlet called "A Parent's Guide to School Nutrition Services." Having decided long ago to pack my children's lunches, I
almost threw it away, but being curious, I glanced over it.

I was shocked. The pamphlet's purpose wasn't simply to inform
parents about the school lunch program; it was designed to discourage parents from making their children a home-packed meal.
The pamphlet reassured parents that "school meals are more eco-
nomical and they provide the best value from both a nutritional

and cost viewpoint." It proclaimed, *without citation*, "...Research has demonstrated that school meals proved more nutrition than typical meals brought from home."

It was this statement "research shows" that really stuck in my craw. To what "research" were school officials referring? What study has determined that home-packed meals are more expensive? What data shows school-provided meals are healthier? They didn't say. They just assumed that we'd all take their word for it, that some other smart person knows better than we do.

This has become a common tactic when someone wants to make a point or win an argument: Use the phrase "studies say" or "research shows," even when it doesn't. In fact, at the time of this writing, a simple Google search of the term "studies say" resulted in 397 million hits. The term "research shows" resulted in 893 million hits.

The good news is women seem to understand what's happening. According to a poll released by the Independent Women's Forum in May 2013, 87 percent of women believe it is cheap and easy to find somebody to argue a given position. That's a hopeful sign that women aren't easily fooled. Yet it betrays a bigger and growing problem: Women don't know which sources to trust. Given the increasing use of official-looking alarmist studies, it's no wonder women are swimming in a sea of uncertainty.

Next up, I provide three quick case studies that provide a window into how "studies" are used and misused by the alarmism industry.

MENU LABELING SHOULD BE LABELED "INEFFECTIVE"

In May 2010, the White House Task Force on Childhood Obesity issued a report to the President with recommendations on how to stem the upward trend of obesity in America.[58] Among the recommendations was requiring restaurants to post calories on their menus (this requirement had been included in the Affordable Care Act, which the President signed into law a few months earlier). To support the recommendation, the task force cited a new study that showed menu labeling helped customers make lower calorie choices.[59] The Task Force's report said this of the study:

> A recent study showed that both information and convenience can have a beneficial effect on how customers choose their meals. The study indicates that when presented with calorie information (how many calories are contained in each menu item) and a calorie recommendation (how many calories men and women of varying activity levels should consume), people on average order meals with significantly fewer calories. Indeed, the effect of providing this information reduced meals by almost 100 calories. The study also showed that making healthier meal choices more convenient has a significant impact on consumption decisions. For example, if healthier options are featured on a menu page and other options require a more active choice, it is likely that fast-food customers will order lower calorie meals.[60]

Sounds pretty convincing, right? After all, this study was cited in a White House report. If that doesn't give a study that whiff of legitimacy, I'm not sure what will.

Yet, when I decided to actually read the study they were citing, I soon realized that it was laughably small. It included only

292 participants and was conducted in only one Subway sandwich shop. More damning, most of the participants were adult, middle-class, white males many of whom admitted currently dieting. That's hardly an accurate representation of the general population.

Of course, the White House conveniently failed to cite a much larger study on menu labeling. That study, published in the *Journal of Health Affairs* a year before the White House report was released (and therefore available to the writers), was conducted by researchers at New York University and Yale University and included over 1,100 customers at four fast-food restaurants (McDonald's, Wendy's, Burger King and Kentucky Fried Chicken).[61] The researchers specifically chose to conduct their surveys in low-income, minority neighborhoods of New York City. Those are areas which have higher rates of obesity, and are therefore among the primary groups the menu labeling effort would hope to impact.

The NYU/Yale study found that only half the customers noticed the calorie counts, which were prominently posted on menu boards. Of those, only 28 percent said the information had influenced their ordering. Nine out of 10 of those who said they had taken the calorie information into account reported that they had made healthier choices as a result. That may sound like a decent result, but upon inspection of their receipts, researchers found that these same customers who said they made healthier choices actually ordered items that were *higher* in calories than the average customer.[62]

The researchers put it succinctly when they said of the study's results: "Simply displaying information about the caloric value of various food options may fail to translate into attitudinal, motivational, or—most importantly—behavioral changes in line with choosing healthier food options."[63]

Let me put it another way. People aren't dumb. Most know they're probably going to eat a high-calorie meal when they walk into a fast food restaurant. They don't need the actual numbers posted on the menu to realize they'll be taking up a big chunk of their daily calorie allowance if they order a double-patty burger topped with bacon and cheese. Other studies have since confirmed my "people aren't stupid" theory:

+ 2011: Duke-NUS Graduate Medical School Study published in the *American Journal for Preventative Medicine* found that calorie counts on menus did not affect people's food decisions. The lead researcher even said that "[G]iven the results of prior studies, we expected the results to be small... but we were surprised that we could not detect even the slightest hint of changes in purchasing behavior..."[64]

+ 2011: NYU's School of Medicine, examined the eating habits of teens and found that menu labels have little effect on their (and their parents') food choices. [65]

Interestingly, the most recent study on menu labeling, released in July 2013, marks a return to the subject from same team of researchers who conducted that small study in one Subway sandwich shop (the study cited by the White House Task Force on Childhood Obesity). In their latest and much larger study, which was published in the *American Journal of Public Health*, the researchers reversed course, finding that calorie information did nothing to help consumers choose healthier menu items.[66]

Lead researcher Julie Downs, an associate research professor of social and decision sciences at Carnegie Melon University's Dietrich

College of Humanities and Social Sciences lamented the study's findings, saying:

> There have been high hopes that menu labeling could be a key tool to help combat high obesity levels in this country, and many people do appreciate having that information available. Unfortunately, this approach doesn't appear to be helping to reduce consumption very much, even when we give consumers what policymakers thought might help: some guidance for how many calories they should be eating.[67]

Science informs. But now, unfortunately and with more regularity, science is being misused to misinform. The costs are high. Thanks to the false impression given to the American public and policymakers that menu labeling would help Americans lose weight, we now have a federal regulation requiring restaurants to spend money labeling the food they offer to consumers. For what?

TEENY, TINY STUDIES MAKE BIG, BAD HEADLINES

Last year, a study published in the journal *NeuroToxicology* made headlines by claiming humans were becoming exposed to two chemicals (phthalates and bisphenol-A) through common "lifestyle behaviors" including eating food bought at the grocery store, using deodorant, soaps and shampoo, and driving cars.[68] The study's authors compared the urine samples of women living in an Old Order Mennonite (OOM) community to women who participated in The National Health and Nutrition Examination Survey (Commonly known as NHANES, this CDC survey examines a nationally representative sample of about 5,000 persons each year, located in counties across the country, 15 of which are visited each year—in other words, a good sampling of the general population).[69]

The study's results (you might want to sit down for this shocking bit of news) showed that women in the OOM community (again, women who live without modern conveniences) had lower levels of chemicals in their bodies than the women in the general population (you know, like women who drive cars and use deodorant).[70]

The reaction was predictable. The *New York Times* published an editorial telling people to "Eat Like a Mennonite."[71] WebMD told women that the "Mennonite Community Study Suggests Link Between Simple Life, Lower BPA Levels."[72] The study also generated headlines at United Press International, Businessweek, and other online publications and blogs.

Yet, there was very little attention to the question of whether elevated levels of chemicals in the NHANES women meant they were less healthy or whether, conversely, living like a menonnite would actually improve the average person's health. I mean, if I'm going to turn away from modern convenieces and live like a mennonite, I at least want to know I'm getting something in return, right?

It isn't hard to understand why this wasn't discussed. Living like an Old Order Mennnonite might reduce the already hard to detect residues of chemicals in your body, but there is no reason to conclude that it will mean that you live longer. In fact, according to one study (and there aren't many studies on Old Order Mennonite communities), "non-OOMs were found to experience better physical health than OOMs..." and "OOM men and women may face health risks due to low incomes, offspring out-migrations and health service usage."[73]

This big omission of why we should care about the presence of trace chemicals or if those traces impact health outcome wasn't the only flaw in the study:

1. The study only included ten women from one OOM commu-
    nity in New York State. Yes, that means you could fit all the
    study's participants into a passenger van (and you could
    pick them up on one street corner because they all lived in
    the same town!). One hardly needs to explain why this com-
    promises the study's legitimacy but if you need a refresher,
    see Question #2 in Chapter 4.

2. The study was designed to generate the results the re-
    searchers sought. The researchers admitted that they chose
    individuals that adhere to a simpler lifestyle, saying that
    members of the OOM community have "a simpler lifestyle
    than the general U.S. population. They grow most of their
    own food, do not apply pesticides, consume few processed
    foods, use many fewer household chemicals and personal
    care products, and depend on automobiles for transporta-
    tion much less than the general population." This descrip-
    tion therefore provides a pretty good explanation of why
    OOM have lower levels of chemicals in their bodies—be-
    cause members of this community avoid plastic products
    and the kind of products that contain chemicals.

3. The study's participants were only asked to provide urine
    samples over a 48-hour period. That simply isn't long
    enough to adequately study the impact of a product or
    chemical on the human body. See Question #3 in Chapter 4.

4. The lead researcher, Shanna Swan, Ph.D. is a known, and
    admitted, anti-chemical activist. Her research has been dis-
    missed by The National Toxicology Program (a government
    office charged with coordinating toxicology research and
    testing) and considered so bad that her "expert" testimony
    has been dismissed as inadmissible in several court cases.

See Question #1 in Chapter 4 for a reminder on why it's important to consider who is behind a scientific study.

Tiny, scientifically dubious studies like these will continue to be cited by activists who can rely on nervous mommy bloggers, scientifically illiterate members of the mainstream press, and those ubiquitous "I-get-paid-to-look-concerned" newscasters to spread these types of scary stories. But reasonable moms should confidently dismiss the alarmism they create and understand them for what they are: make-believe stories meant to indimidate you. Don't take the bait and for heaven's sake, don't start living like you're a character in Little House on the Prairie in the hopes of living a healthier life.

A DIET OF GENETICALLY MODIFIED FEAR...

One area in which the alarmists have been remarkably effective is in scaring the wits out of the American public about genetically modified organisms (GMO).

Ahhh! Frankenfood. It's ALIVE!

Alarmists tell Americans that they should avoid GMOs for a variety of terrifying reasons. They say GMOs causes cancer, deadly allergic reactions, insect and weed resistance, or, my personal favorite, the catchall claim that GM food poses "unknown risks" to humans.

Yeah, the GMO alarmists love to tell a scary story, but they have a real and growing problem: The alarmists cannot point to one study to support their outrageous claims of grave danger posed by GMOs. Worse still for the alarmists, there are literally hundreds of studies that show genetically modified (GM) food to be safe for human consumption.[74]

In addition to these studies, consider the fact that consumers spend around 90 cents of every dollar on processed foods, most of which contain genetically modified corn and soybeans.[75] That means, a majority of Americans are munching away on GM food right now and have been since it began appearing in the marketplace in the 1990s. And they should continue to do so worry free. But if that doesn't reassure you, consider these facts:

✦ As of this writing, more than 600 peer-reviewed studies confirm that there's nothing scary about genetically modified food. Of course, people can dismiss these many studies by claiming they were all paid for by "big agriculture," but in fact, around 30 percent of the studies were conducted by independent scientists. [76]

✦ A meta-study of 24 separate studies (examining five generations) found that GM food is not a health hazard to humans. The study also found that the difference between GM and conventionally grown food is "not statistically significant."[77]

✦ In 2001, European Union research commissioner Philippe Busquin declared that after fifteen years of tests in 400 European laboratories, the EU had not found "any new risks to human health or the environment, beyond the usual uncertainties of conventional plant breeding."[78]

✦ A 2011 EU review of 81 separate European studies of genetically modified organisms found no evidence that GM food poses any new risks to human health or the environment.[79]

✦ In May 2012, the European Food Safety Authority rejected a proposed ban on GM corn saying, "...there is no specific scientific evidence, in terms of risk to human and animal health or the environment."[80]

✦ These separate studies have been supported by scientific and medical organizations around the world, including the

American Medical Association, the World Health Organization, the UN's Food & Agriculture Organization, the Institute
for Food Technologists and the American Dietetic Association, the U.S. Food and Drug Administration (FDA), the
European Food Safety Authority (EFSA) and Food Safety
Commission of Japan (FSCJ).

Given the preponderance of evidence in favor of the safety of GM
food coupled with the complete lack of evidence of danger, it
makes sense that anti-GMO forces are desperate to produce a body
of scientific research that demonstrates the heretofore-unproven
claim that GM food is harmful. That desperation has led to some
pretty sloppy research and the promotion of the junk science that
purports to demonstrate GM harm.

For example, in the fall of 2012, GM alarmists announced they
finally had the proof they so desperately desired. A new study, conducted by French researcher Gilles-Eric Seralini from the University
of Caen, claimed that rats fed a diet of GM corn died earlier than
those on a non-GM diet. Reuters reported:[81]

> In Rats fed a lifetime diet of Monsanto's genetically
> modified corn or exposed to its top-selling weed killer
> Roundup suffered tumours and multiple organ damage,
> according to a French study published on Wednesday.
>
> Although the lead researcher's past record as a
> critic of the industry may make other experts wary
> of drawing hasty conclusions, the finding will stoke
> controversy about the safety of GM crops.
>
> In an unusual move, the research group did not
> allow reporters to seek outside comment on their

paper before its publication in the peer-reviewed journal *Food and Chemical Toxicology* and presentation at a news conference in London.

Gilles-Eric Seralini of the University of Caen and colleagues said rats fed on a diet containing NK603 — a seed variety made tolerant to dousings of Roundup — or given water containing Roundup at levels permitted in the United States died earlier than those on a standard diet.

The animals on the GM diet suffered mammary tumours, as well as severe liver and kidney damage.[82]

To accompany the study's publication, Seralini loaded a spooky video on YouTube showing blue surgical scrub-wearing researchers holding tumor-riddled rats up to the camera; creepy music played in the background and a British-accented voice asked: "Will we finally know the truth about GMOs? Would we then be faced with a health crisis of global proportions?"[83]

It made good theater.

Following the study's and video's release, mommy blogs as well as the mainstream media exploded with alarmist claims that the Seralini study proved GM food was harmful (as of this writing, I saw reference to the Seralini study on my own Facebook newsfeed). Celebrity doctor and daytime television host (and Oprah bestie) Dr. Oz dedicated a show to GM food alarmism (Dr. Oz's wife is a well-known anti-GMO activist) where he invited a notorious anti-GMO activist (with no scientific background) as an expert guest to discuss this complicated scientific issue.[84]

Naturally, people were worried and their fear was supported by the mainstream media, which cited the Seralini study as definitive proof of GM food's toxicity. But fear and uncertainty weren't the only byproduct of the Seralini study. The hysteria had real consequences. Shortly after the study's release, French Prime Minister Jean-Marc Ayrault announced that if the results were confirmed, the government would press for a Europe-wide ban on GM corn. The European Commission instructed the independent European Food Safety Agency (EFSA) in Parma, Italy, to assess the study and the Russian government temporarily suspended importing GM corn.

In an even more dramatic turn, the government of Kenya banned all GM crops. Anti-GMO forces called the Kenyan government's move a victory.[85] One wonders how the 1.1 million Kenyans suffering from hunger feel about this win.[86]

Yet, despite the alarmism and the premature actions of these regulatory bodies, in only a matter of weeks (and a full month before Kenya banned GMOs), the certainty began to crumble.[87] On October 19, 2012, six French scientific academies issued a statement on Seralini's study. Agence France-Presse reported at the time that the scientists called the Seralini study a "scientific non-event," and added:[88]

> "This work does not enable any reliable conclusion to be drawn," they said, adding bluntly that the affair helped "spread fear among the public."
>
> The joint statement—an extremely rare event in French science—was signed by the national academies of agriculture, medicine, pharmacy, sciences, technology and veterinary studies.
>
> It was sparked by research published in September that said rats fed with so-called NK603 corn and/or doses of Roundup herbicide developed tumours.

The paper, led by Gilles-Eric Seralini at the University of Caen, unleashed a storm in Europe, where GM crops are a highly sensitive issue.

Critics accused Seralini of manipulating the media to boost the impact of his findings, branded his experiments as shoddy or fraught with gaps or bias.

Two fast-track official investigations into the study, ordered by the government, are due to be unveiled on Monday.

The academies' statement said:

"Given the numerous gaps in methods and interpretation, the data presented in this article cannot challenge previous studies which have concluded that NK603 corn is harmless from the health point of view, as are, more generally, genetically modified plants that have been authorised for consumption by animals and humans."

It does bewilder that today the Seralini study is still cited as a study that demonstrates the danger of GM food. But it's understandable. There simply isn't any good science out there showing harm from eating genetically modified food. What's an alarmist to do but use the most recent junk science to plead their case?

CHAPTER 6

THE DANGER OF FICKLE SCIENCE
(OR IS ANYONE LISTENING ANYMORE?)

83% OF WOMEN HAVE TROUBLE DISTINGUISHING ALARMIST HEADLINES FROM VALID WARNINGS ABOUT HARMFUL FOOD OR HOUSEHOLD PRODUCTS
- IAF POLL

Independent attitudes *forums*   ALARMISM   IWF.ORG

* *

*I*n 2006, when I was pregnant with my first child, my doctor told me to avoid tuna fish because of the mercury that fish flesh contained due to industrial pollution. This was no small sacrifice for me. Tuna was a staple in my diet. I ate it on a regular basis as sushi, in salads, on sandwiches. But it wasn't just my doctor telling me to lay-off my favorite food. The Internet was rife with stories warning women that the mercury in fish could harm a growing baby.

I didn't mind making the change. In fact, I went overboard, totally eliminating tuna and all other fish from my diet. I remember feeling proud of my sacrifice since I believed I was doing it to ensure my baby's health and safety.

Well, imagine my annoyance when only a few years later, doctors and medical researchers reversed their prior advice. Today, women are told to *eat*, not avoid, tuna and other fish because of the brain-boosting omega-3 fatty acids fish contains. In other words— eating fish was good for a baby's brain. As for those mercury claims: A recent study that spans a whopping 30 years found no association between mercury exposure while pregnant and autism-like behaviors in children.[89]

Oops! I guess my poor first born will someday blame me when he gets lower grades then his younger brothers. Sorry, kid!

You'd think these types of alarmist claims would diminish with each debunking. Yet, it seems just the opposite is true. In fact, the alarmism appears to be getting more and more outlandish. The latest example involves not the food pregnant women might be ingesting, but the chemicals with which they might come into contact when carrying junior.

These latest warnings don't just involve telling pregnant women to lay-off such obviously dangerous activities as spraying insecticide in the backyard or re-tarring a driveway. These warnings—issued by the British Royal College of Obstetricians and Gynecologists—say women "should be made aware of the sources and routes of chemical exposure in order to minimize harm to their unborn child" and recommends "that the best approach for pregnant women is a 'safety first' approach, which is to assume there is risk present even when it may be minimal or eventually unfounded."[90]

In other words, the British Royal College wants women to abide by the precautionary principle which holds that since we don't know, we should react to everything with caution and alarm in anticipation that at some point (in a year, a decade, a century, millennia?) a product will be found to be harmful. Wow. That sounds like a fabulous way to live. How about we just wrap women in cellophane and put them in a padded room when they announce a pregnancy?

Specifically, the Royal College tells women to:

✦ Use fresh food and reduce canned food and food containers in plastic bags (I guess low-income women should just forgo the healthy frozen and canned options that come at a much lower price than fresh vegetables).

✦ Minimize the use of cosmetics and moisturizers (because we already feel super pretty with all that extra poundage we're carrying around).

✦ Minimize the purchase of newly produced household furniture and fabrics (well, I guess this dresser drawer will make a nice crib and we can just pile all the new clothes on the floor. No woop).

✦ Avoid non-stick pans (because who doesn't want to go out and purchase a whole new set of full-stick pans when we're already saving for baby).

✦ Avoid air fresheners (because that lingering vomit smell is great during that first trimester).

✦ Minimize the use of home cleaning products (because a dirty living environment and germs are totally fine for my growing baby).

The medical officials in charge of this report admitted that they "erred on the side of caution" (ya think?) but defended it on the basis that they wanted to warn people of potential dangers (then why no mention of alien attacks and asteroids? It could happen!).

Yet, what the authors failed to understand is that reports like this one create a real danger for pregnant women: The anxiety generated by the suggestion that every single thing that surrounds you when you're pregnant isn't good for babies in utero. In fact, there are lasting consequences of this alarmism.

Recent research published in the journal *Development and Psychopathology* found that pregnant women who experienced common stressful events during pregnancy had an increased risk of behavioral problems in the children they carried while stressed.[91] Researchers at the University of Edinburgh found that pregnant women who suffer stress during pregnancy can give birth to children more prone to depression and anxiety.[92] And in a 2010 study, researchers found that the stress experienced by a mother can affect the brain development of the fetus.[93]

In addition, alarmist reports like this force expectant mothers to concentrate on these non-issues rather than focusing on their nutrition and other healthy habits, like moderate exercise, adequate sleep and other things that will ensure their baby is born alive and healthy. Reports like this also make it a lot less fun to be pregnant. Who wants to be pregnant if you are constantly worrying that you're systematically killing your baby every time you fry an egg or wash your hair?

Likely, we'll soon see a reversal of this report's suggestions. And the women who were warned to stay away from these common products will feel annoyed that they were ever given this silly advice in the first place. But they'll also feel betrayed and angry, and they'll likely meet with skepticism the next alarmist report to make headlines. What's more troubling, these moms might just tune out the legitimate warnings which could ultimately harm them. These are the costs of fickle recommendations based on dubious science.

Pregnant women aren't the only ones targeted. Lovers of salty snack foods have also had to deal with the schizophrenic health warnings. In 2011, three powerful regulatory agencies — the Food and Drug Administration, the Department of Agriculture, and the Department of Health and Human Services – began accepting comments on "approaches to reducing sodium consumption." The goal was to reduce sodium consumption from the average 3,400 milligrams a day (approximately 1.5 teaspoons) to what the current dietary guidelines recommend which is 2,300 for the general population and 1,500 for those with health risks such as older Americans, African-Americans, and people with high blood pressure, diabetes or chronic kidney disease.

The most troublesome part of these agencies' request was that the request itself cited wildly outdated and even inaccurate information about salt's connection to poor health and heart disease. This wasn't because they were unfamiliar with the new studies that contradict the idea that lower salt intake is key to improving health outcomes; the agency simply ignored the studies in conflict with their regulatory goals.

Among the studies that contradicted the agency's claims was a 2011 European study involving 3,700 participants who were examined for eight years. That study concluded that those who had the lowest sodium diets had the highest mortality rates.[94] Other studies had similar conclusions. A 2006 study published in the *American Journal of Medicine,* which included 78 million Americans, found the more sodium people consumed, the less likely they were to die from heart disease.[95] That's right: Those who ingested more salt had healthier hearts than those who consumed less. A 2007 study published in the *European Journal of Epidemiology* found no association between the amount of salt in the participant's diets and the risk of death from cardiovascular disease.[96] Some researchers even began to warn of the dangers of promoting a low-salt diet for millions of otherwise-healthy Americans.[97]

Even the relationship between salt and hypertension was being questioned. A study published in the science journal *Nature* suggested genetics, not diet, contributes more to hypertension.[98] Yet another study suggested obesity, not salt, determined an individual's blood pressure.[99] And a 2013 study from the University of California, Davis, followed the sodium consumption habits of 70,000 participants from 45 countries over 50 years and found that people's brains work to automatically adjust the amount of salt in their diets—which is similar to how other animals regulate salt consumption.[100]

Due to the overwhelmingly negative reaction to the government's plans to regulate salt and the clear research that put into question the sodium-heart disease link, in 2013, the CDC asked the U.S. Institute of Medicine (IOM) to review all of the various salt studies. Shortly after, the IOM released its findings, saying that while it might be a good idea for all Americans to lower their salt intake, there was no evidence that lowering it across the board (as the regulators wanted to do) will benefit the health of Americans, and for some subgroups, these lowered sodium levels might lead to adverse health effects.[101]

So, what should the average person (and government regulators) take away from all these varied and disparate studies on salt's impact on the human body? The conclusion is clear: The science simply isn't settled on salt. Therefore, individual people with the help of their own doctors—not government regulators—need to make decisions about salt's role in their own diets.

While one might be quick to blame the medical community for these ever-changing health opinions, the real culprit is the media eager to make a headline. The reality is, researchers and the medical community need to publish their findings. But it's the media that fails to put many of these new studies into perspective. For instance, one press report might detail the latest findings of a study without pointing out that other studies say the opposite. That's frustrating for the media consumer who may see contradictory health advice and not know what to make of it.

The best thing consumers can do is to consult with professionals paid to keep up on the latest research. Ignore the scary headlines and talk to your doctor. It doesn't matter if you're a pregnant woman or a 60-year-old man dealing with hypertension, you and your doctor are the best authorities on your health.

PART III

....

THE EXPENSIVE "SOLUTIONS" TO ALARMISM

... one of the single most important things we can do to fight childhood obesity is to make those meals at school as healthy and nutritious as possible.
—Michelle Obama, *Speech before the School Nutrition Association, 2010*[102]

CHAPTER 7

OUR OBESE GOVERNMENT IS GOBBLING US UP

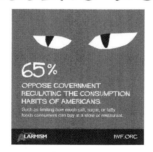

Taking my oldest son to the store to pick out his first lunch box was a big moment for me. It was the first school-related chore I'd done with my firstborn and I admit I got a little teary eyed watching him enthusiastically pick out his red and blue firefighter-themed lunch box.

I remember doing this with my mom—the yearly trek to K-mart to get back-to-school clothes (yeah, I was stylish in my K-mart duds), my pink Trapper Keeper and spiral notebooks, pencils, pens, and whatever else was on the long list. I also remember—oddly, quite clearly—the crushing pressure I felt trying to decide between the Princess Leia and the Little House on the Prairie lunch box.

Hey! These things mattered!

Today, one of these items is no longer on many parents shopping list: More and more kids don't need a little box to contain the meal their parents lovingly (or in my case on most mornings, not-so-lovingly) packed for them. Simply put, school feeding programs have grown to become a massive government entitlement program that feed not just poor and working-class children, but any kid who wants to eat on the lunch line (and what kid wouldn't when they are serving—and continue to serve—pizza and chicken nuggets?). Relying on what's being served at school has become the preferred method of feeding children in this country.

In fact, school feeding programs have become so ingrained in our culture, that today, it is utterly possible for a child to be fed entirely outside his or her home. The scenario makes sense: Upon waking, many children are dropped off at a daycare facility or at school (most schools have a program called "before care"), where they are served breakfast. When lunch rolls around, that child will be provided a noon-time school meal, and thanks to another expansion made by the Obama Administration in 2011, dinner will be served to many school children as well.

It wasn't always this way. The school lunch program began in 1946 when it served a comparatively modest 7 million kids, all of who lived in poverty. Today, even as Americans have become wealthier and children are healthier and better fed than any other time in history, feeding programs designed to help poor and undernourished children have experienced rapid growth—and now feed children well above the poverty line.

In fact, of the roughly five billion meals served during the 2011-12 school year, a third of those were paid in full, which means a significant portion of the kids in the school lunch line either don't need or fail to qualify for a free or reduced cost meal. The question is: Why is a program designed to feed poor and undernourished kids being used by millions of middle class families?

Some argue that it's still cheaper to eat a school lunch but even on a per-lunch cost comparison, school lunches (which cost on average $2.08) still come at a higher price than the average home cooked meal (the meals I pack for my kids come in around $1.80 per meal and many other mom bloggers report similar or smaller amounts).

So, if it isn't need-based, what is driving the expansion of these feeding programs?

One reason is our culture of alarmism, which government officials use as a tool to convince parents that their children will really be better off being fed by the "experts" at the school rather than stupid old mom and dad. In the government's view, it's far better to turn your children over to your friendly government minders who have a far, far better sense of what's best for kids. To get parents to roll over and send little Johnny off to school lunch-free, parents are actively discouraged from packing their kids lunch.

Getting more kids into the lunch line has been promoted as the key to tackling the childhood obesity problem, which the First Lady claimed as her signature issue shortly after her husband took office. Mrs. Obama quickly jumped on board with the alarmists, saying in 2010 that "[T]he surge in obesity in this country is nothing short of a public health crisis that is threatening our children, our families, and our future," adding that "the health consequences are so severe that medical experts have warned that our children could be on track to live shorter lives than their parents" and that "we do not have a moment to waste."[103] That same year, the First Lady said she sympathized with local Mayors who had to deal with their less productive, overweight workers.[104] And in December 2010, she went further, suggesting, during a speech to schoolchildren, that obesity was the greatest national security threat facing the country.[105]

Health and Human Services Secretary Kathleen Sebelius also joined the alarmist game saying that childhood obesity would cause the current generation to live shorter lives than their parents.[106] And in perhaps the best example of government officials spewing alarmist gobbledygook, former head of the CDC Julie Gerberding said the obesity "epidemic" was worse than the black plague—that 13th century worldwide pandemic that reduced Europe's population by a full 50 percent in two years (think mass graves!).[107]

With such a tremendous threat to our very nation's survival, it's no wonder people began to believe that government intervention was needed in order to arrest the crisis! Expanding the school lunch program as well as green lighting new regulations on food companies, clamping down on the use of certain ingredients, and strongarming restaurants into making changes to their menus, all seem like merely modest intrusions into the free market and our personal lives given so great a threat.

But these aren't just modest intrusions. They are significant. Okay, maybe each one taken alone isn't terribly significant or costly, but taken together they are fundamentally transforming our society for the worse. All the regulations on food providers add up to higher grocery bills and fewer jobs (as I'll describe more in Chapter 9).

Taxpayers lose more than $18 billion dollars to a variety of school feeding programs. This $18 billion doesn't just fund the lunch program (although that still came in at a hefty $11.4 billion for fiscal year 2012). It funds other feeding and food commodity programs, such as the school breakfast program, the summer feeding program, the special milk program, childcare and afterschool feeding programs and the fresh fruit program, which provides schools grants for purchasing fresh produce for school kids.

But for Washington politicians, three squares a day, five days a week, served at the local school isn't enough. In 2013, House Democrats proposed legislation expanding school feeding programs to weekends and holidays.[108] I mean, what child doesn't dream of eating Thanksgiving dinner at school?

The economics of the movement to transfer responsibility for feeding kids from parents to the government isn't what bothers me most: The real problem is the damage done to the idea of limited government and personal responsibility. What can parents be trusted to do if not to make a sandwich for their kids?

This is a symptom of a larger problem in America, as we let government grow explosively into every facet of our lives—snooping through our records and monitoring our habits—because of the idea that without their constant oversight we couldn't make it on our own. Is this really how Americans see themselves?

In my own conversations with people on this subject, I'm often gobsmacked by the charge that I don't care about poor kids. Others patiently try to remind me that "parents just aren't what they used to be" and that "parents simply don't have the time and can't afford to prepare simple meals for their children anymore." These somewhat patronizing arguments always strike me as complete nonsense given the many other forms of food assistance out there to help families who live under the poverty line. From food stamps (now called SNAP which stands for the Supplemental Nutrition Assistance Program) to programs designed for seniors and women with infants, there is ample federal food assistance designed to make sure people can afford adequate groceries. Heck, there are even programs designed to help poor and elderly people shop at foodie-approved farmers markets.

And the fact is that many poor parents do step up and prepare food for their children. For instance, a January 2012 report by anti-hunger organization Share Our Strength demonstrated that low-income Americans work hard to cook for their families. Specifically, the report showed that 8 in 10 low-income families make dinner at home and from scratch at least five times a week. Families only eat fast food on average one night a week and that while some families do struggle to cook healthy meals every night, an impressive 85 percent of these families said they wanted to make healthy meals and believe eating healthy is realistic for them.[109]

Yet, today, the government is sending parents the message that they shouldn't bother and that they should just let the government takeover meal preparation for their children. This is the wrong message for improving children's health. Ms. Obama, as a mother, instinctively knows this. When she shared her own experience as a parent dealing with her daughters' weight fluctuations, she explained the steps she'd taken to help them develop better habits—switching to skim milk and healthier snacks, sitting down to dinner and turning off the television. She didn't push Malia and Sasha into a government cafeteria so that the lunch lady could stick some carrots on their plate, which they would then go toss in the trash can. She knew that she needed to lead the way in helping her daughters.

Yet the First Lady has little faith in Americans to take similar steps. Instead of encouraging parents to make similar changes in their own households, she wants the government to take the lead in helping kids lose weight and stay healthy. Addressing the School Nutrition Association in 2010, she hinted at a big-government solution saying "...one of the single most important things we can do to fight childhood obesity is to make those meals at school as healthy and nutritious as possible."[110]

The solution, therefore, wasn't for parents to follow the First Lady's excellent example; it was to grow government by expanding the school lunch program. By telling Americans to "do as I say" (eat government-provided food from the cafeteria), "not as I do" (pay attention to what your children are eating and make appropriate changes), Ms. Obama missed a golden opportunity to help parents understand the critical role they play in their children's health and to address and discuss childhood obesity as it should be—as a very personal and individual problem.

In 2010, and with the help of the First Lady, Congress passed the Healthy, Hunger Free Kids Act—a bill that added billions to the USDA program and further marginalized parents by expanding the direct-certification program. By authorizing schools to snoop into state Medicaid records, children receiving those state benefits could be automatically enrolled in school feeding programs. Why is this significant? It might seem minor, but it takes away the process by which parents used to actually enroll their children in these feeding programs, by actually going to the school to sign up their kids. By making this process automatic, parents are again marginalized— their role in deciding how and what their children eat becomes superfluous.

This is in direct contradiction to what the latest research says is critical to children reducing and maintaining a healthy weight. A 2010 study by Ohio State University found that only three activities help reduce childhood obesity: eating dinner at home with your family, watching less television, and getting enough sleep at night.[111] These are all basic parental responsibilities that are whittled away as government increasingly takes over the role of feeding young chilren. And since the bill requires states to show that they are actively working to increase enrollment rates, states now have an incentive to ignore this important research and proceed with enrolling as many kids as possible in school feeding programs. Clearly the purpose is to grow government, not to make kids healthier.

The First Lady would have better served the American public if she had started telling parents to practice some pretty basic habits: Make your kids a lunch. Sit down to dinner. Turn off the television, and put your kids to bed at a reasonable hour. But that's not the tact government—or the alarmists—want to take.

CHAPTER 8

SCARING AWAY SAFE AND HEALTHY PRODUCTS

· ·

A few times each week, I take my three very young sons to the grocery store. It can be a bit chaotic as I try to load the grocery cart while both watching the kids and averting my eyes from those other customers who think I'm either cracked or drunk for attempting to shop with three little boys aged six and under. I've learned to be quick. I know what I need and, most days, can make it out of the store without much drama.

Yet, it isn't just my shopping skills that make for successful kid-in-tow trips to the store. Much of the ease of shopping today comes because food manufacturers have tapped into the busy mom demographic.

Let me be clear, this chapter isn't a love story to big agriculture, corporate food giants or processed food, but it is a reminder to moms that we sure do have it comparatively good and certainly better than our own moms had it when it comes to what's available for caring for our families. From individually wrapped cheese sticks and single serving applesauce to all sorts of bagged and pre-washed greens and frozen vegetables and neatly trimmed, single-serving chicken breasts, food manufacturers are thankfully listening to you and me. They heard moms say "please, make things easier." Moms should applaud this progress.

Yet, there is a downside to this convenience. As food production in America has increasingly become automated, industrialized and hidden from view, people are increasingly ignorant about food production and that nurtures another human condition—constant alarmism and anxiety about the food we eat. People are naturally weary of things they know nothing about and therefore, the modern home cook, with all her convenient prepackaged products, has become easily rattled by the rather unappetizing reality of food production. For instance, many are shocked when hearing about the less-than-happy world at the animal slaughterhouse.

The public's ignorance of meat production is understandable in our modern world, but it's important that people make the distinction between things that are actually dangerous and things that are merely unpleasant. Alarmists prey on these misunderstandings to push their agenda—and often with serious consequences.

Consider, for instance, the recent firestorm over a meat product commonly called "pink slime." The manufactured alarmism about this product had very real and unfortunate consequences. It resulted in terrified consumers, fewer jobs, and most concerning, a less-safe food supply.

Let me first dispel a few myths about pink slime. First, it isn't slime; it is meat. Technically called Lean Finely Textured Beef (LFTB), the product is simply small, very lean pieces of beef that have been removed from an animal during the butchering process. Interestingly, the process was first introduced in the 1980s as a way to provide Americans with less expensive ground beef products. *USA Today* offered a tidy history lesson on the product:[112]

> In the early 1990s, Eldon Roth, a savvy Midwest entrepreneur, came up with a way to turn meat trimmings into profit. He heated them, spun them in a centrifuge to separate the tiny particles of meat from fat, then treated the product with a puff of ammonium hydroxide gas to kill bacteria. It became known in the industry as "lean, finely textured beef," or LFTB, and Roth made a fortune selling frozen bricks of it to add to ground beef. It makes the beef cheaper and leaner.[113]

Look, I get it. There's no doubt that pink slime rates high on the gag meter, but the product isn't dangerous. In fact, it's an extremely lean protein source, coming in around 98 percent fat free. Aren't we supposed to be lowering the amount of animal fats in our diets? Unfortunately, for the public, the media focused more on the slime and less on the healthy quality of the product.

That's precisely what happened in March 2012 when ABC News ran a story on "pink slime." At the time of the ABC program, LFBT was present in 70 percent of ground beef products sold in the United States.[114] Much of it was sent to schools to be used in the school lunch program. Naturally, ABC news wanted ratings and this was a classic ratings grab with the report's outraged whistleblowers, shocked and panicked consumers, as well as suggestions (yet no actual proof) of criminal behavior on the part of a former USDA official and the beef industry.

The story generated dozens of copycat reports and calls for changes in the beef industry. Demand to end the use of LFTB was swift. Schools began lobbying to purchase pink slime-free beef, grocery chains whipped up marketing strategies, and fast food and other big restaurant chains claimed they weren't using the stuff (What, us? No way!). PR Daily even listed the "pink slime" controversy in its online list of worse PR disasters of 2012.[115] Meanwhile, LFTB plants were forced to shut down and over a thousand workers were laid off in the Midwest.

To say this is an over-reaction is an understatement. Even Obama administration appointee Elisabeth Hagan, the USDA's Undersecretary for Food Safety (who also happens to be a physician and mother), endorsed the product, saying, "LFTB is safe and has been used for a very long time. And adding LFTB to ground beef does not make that ground beef any less safe to consume."[116]

Another notable voice, Nancy Donley, president and chief spokesperson for food safety nonprofit STOP Foodborne Illness defends the product. Donley, who tragically lost her six-year old son Alex to E. coli-contaminated ground beef in 1993, is no corporate hack. She's dedicated her life to food safety and has voiced her concern over the "misinformation swirling around the Internet and TV about lean beef produced by Beef Products, Inc. [a LFTB manufacturer]." Donley has officially defended the product and the manufacturers of LFTB, saying:

> I have personally visited their plant and the categorization of calling their product "pink slime" is completely false and incendiary. Consumers need to un-

derstand that this product is meat, period, and that the use of ammonia hydroxide in minute amounts during processing improves the safety of the product and is routinely used throughout the food industry.[117]

ABC News and the other food alarmists complaining about pink slime should take a look at how they used to do it back in the good old days in those idyllic agrarian cultures. Beverly Hungry Wolf, a member of the Blood tribe of the Blackfoot people, was born and raised on the Blood Indian reservation, which is the largest Indian reserve in Canada. In her book *The Ways of my Grandmothers*, she explains how her mother processed whole animals:[118]

One of the first things from the cow that my grandmother prepared was the insides, because they spoil the quickest. Most important of these were the heart, kidney, liver and lungs. The tongue she would just slice open and hang up to dry, and the same with the lungs. The rest were either eaten raw, thrown on the coals and roasted, or boiled and laid out in the sun to dry.

...

If the animal was a female with an unborn young or a suckling, this was fed to the older people, because it was so tender. The meat would be boiled, and the guts would be taken out and braided, and then boiled, too.

...

The animals bones were broken open for the marrow grease...The fat that came out was skimmed off and put in a special container. It turned into something like hard lard.

...

The hooves were boiled down until all the gristle in them was soft...The way I remember those boiled hooves, there was hardly anything worth eating on them. But my grandparents liked them.

...

If the animal was butchered at home by my grandmother, she always used the blood too. A favorite meal was to take about a cup full of blood with a saucerful of flower. This mixture was worked with the fingers until all the clots and lumps broke up. Usually she saved the broth from the boss ribs that she first cooked for my grandfather. She would boil some serviceberies in that broth, then stir in the blood mixture very slowly. She kept stirring it and tasting it until she was satisfied that she had blood soup the way she liked it.

Frances Densmore's book *Chippewa Customs* contains similar description, explaining how the Chippewa people produced their own form of "pink slime:"[119]

The meat of an entire deer was spread in layers on a tanned dear hide and pounded with a board until it was in shreds. It was then thoroughly mixed with hot deer tallow and put in a deer-hide bag. When desired for use it was cut in slices.

> The dried meat was cut in pieces, spread on birch bark, and covered with birch bark. A man then trod on it until with was crushed. This was called by a term meaning "food-trodden meat."

As explained in these testimonials, using every part of the animal isn't unusual. Yet today, merely trimming fresh meat from larger pieces of fat and tissue to be ground and later mixed into ground beef is considered not only unappetizing, but dangerous. We never used to be this squeamish. Americans were tougher, heartier, and more skeptical of snake oils salesman like today's modern media desperate for higher ratings.

While USDA official Hagan's support of the LFTB industry helped quell some of the hysteria surrounding the product, following Avila's series, the USDA gave a nod to the hysteria by announcing it would allow school districts to decide whether to purchase beef that does not contain LFTB. I'm all for the USDA loosening feeding restrictions, but this action was based on political pressure, not a desire to let local schools control the lunch program. This resulted in a tough decision for schools. If they elected to go LFTB-free, they were left with two undesirable choices: cheap, high-fat beef, or expensive, low-fat beef. In other words, if schools gave into the alarmism about LFTB they would have to offer kids fattier, less healthy beef or pay a lot more for LFTB-free, low-fat beef, which means they'd have to take that money out of another part of the budget.

Most schools appear to be opting for the fattier stuff, which should make the food police and obesity scolds squirm. According to USDA data, in 2011, 37 percent of beef sold was the lower-priced fattier ground beef, and now that figure has risen to 48 percent.

Lean ground beef costs 50 cents more per pound today than it did then, and according to the Congressional Research Service, these price hikes are expected to continue.[120] And the decisions made by many retailers to halt the use of LFTB will result in even higher prices for consumers and schools.

Keep this in mind as you hear the next news story about your local school's budget crunch. Part of this is a product of the culture of alarmism. Schools are spending more today on meat products because of trumped up hysteria about a perfectly safe, healthy product.

Schools already jump through ridiculous, costly hoops to protect their students from other so-called risks. Consider the movement to make school playground equipment safe. For years, playgrounds have been designed to remove risks, yet this "can't be too safe" attitude carries with it some unintended consequences.

When Philip Howard, chairman of the legal-reform coalition Common Good, wrote in a *Wall Street Journal* op-ed that too-safe playground equipment was making kids fat, my first reaction was to roll my eyes. Here we go again, I thought, blaming another inanimate object (But, I thought it was the toys in happy meals!) for childhood obesity. Yet, after reading the piece, I realized Howard had a point. Explaining the anger people felt after some children burned their bare feet on playground equipment that had gotten hot under the summer sun, Howard laments that the answer wasn't simply to tell kids to put their dang shoes on.[121] Nope, it was to demand playground redesigns to make them burn proof! From Howard's oped:

> The outrage was immediate. "Playgrounds should
> be designed with canopies," one park- safety advo-
> cate declared. "How many burn cases will it take,"

Betsy Gotbaum, the city's public advocate asked, "before the city wakes up and acts?"

The headlong drive for safety has indeed created dangers, but not those identified by the safety zealots. Risk is important in child development. Allowing children to test their limits in unstructured play, according to the American Association of Pediatrics, "develop[s] their imagination, dexterity, and physical, cognitive, and emotional strength." Scrapes and bruises are how children learn their limits, and the need to take personal responsibility.

The harmful effects of our national safety obsession ripple outward into society. One in six children in America is obese, and many of them will face a lifetime of chronic illness. According to the Center for Disease Control, this problem would basically cure itself if children engaged in the informal outdoor activities that used to be normal. But how do we lure children off the sofa? One key attraction is risk.[122]

Howard goes on to remind us that risk is actually fun. It's fun to feel that rush of adrenalin as you do something a tiny bit dangerous. But risk (and fun) is increasingly disappearing for children as schools try to make things as safe as possible. The outcome is obvious: By removing risk, schools are also removing any lessons kids might get in risk analysis (should I jump from this high platform or make a better decision to climb down the nearby ladder?) as well as making these physically challenging (and calorie burning) activities less desirable. Howard points out that playgrounds have become so boring that they don't attract kids over the age of four:

> Exercise in schools is carefully programmed, when
> it exists at all. Some schools have banned tag. Bro-
> ward County, Fla., banned running at recess. (How
> else can we guard against a child falling down?)
> Little Leagues forbid sliding into base. Some towns
> ban sledding. High diving boards are history, and it's
> only a matter of time before all diving boards disap-
> pear.[123]

I have some experience with what Howard describes. My three children, aged three to six, spend hours each week playing at the school
playground. While my three year old still enjoys the playground's
safe slides and easy-to-tackle climbing structures, my 4 and 6 year
olds wouldn't be caught dead on the boring old playground, which
they claim "is for babies!" Instead, they prefer to spend their time
tromping through the adjacent soccer field, hanging from the low
tree branches, running thought the tic-infested tall grass, and climbing up and around the enormous, mud encrusted root of the gnarly
tree that the school thankfully hasn't yet removed.

While my children are able to find some somewhat risky play
in nature, when I was a child, risky play was actually provided by
the community. In the early 1980s, my mother would take my older sister and me to a small lake where the town maintained not
only a terrifyingly high dive platform (as well as many lower diving
boards), but a huge (and somewhat rickety-looking) wooden slide
contraption called the Sea Dive. With a narrow stairway on one side,
and the slide on the other, kids would climb forty or so feet up to
a walk-in closet sized, railed-in platform and wait, their anticipation
and fear growing. When it was your turn, you'd grab a tray-like seat
and holding on to the sides, slide down the Sea Dive into the murky

lake waters below. I went once, only once—gripping onto my sister's waist so tight, I doubt she bore breath the whole agonizing and utterly petrifying trip down.

I'm glad my sister and I experienced the slide that day because, sadly for all the kids in that tiny farming town where I spent my childhood, the slide was closed a few years later due to fears of injuries and lawsuits.

Not long after the Sea Dive was torn down, the high dive platform was removed. Years later, I heard the bathhouse and snack bar (the summertime social hub of the teen set) burned down and wasn't rebuilt. A childhood friend (who still lives in my hometown) explained that the once-fun lake has "lost its sparkle." She says no one swims there anymore and, while you can still rent paddleboats, "the beach is definitely not what we remember," adding "we had some great times there but it hasn't been that caliber for probably 20 years."

So, what do kids do now during those hot summer months? I suspect quite a few—probably the very ones who would have been jumping off that high dive or screaming down the Sea Dive—now sit inside air conditioned houses playing video games where at least the characters in the game have some excitement in their lives. All the while, kids are piling on the pounds.

Sometimes you have to think a bit to see how some of these safety measures actually backfire in terms of health. Other times it's frighteningly obvious. Take those who want to make us safe from so called "toxic chemicals"—such as the chemicals that act as flame-retardants, which can delay the spread of fire.

Today, flame-retardants are standard in most clothing and have become commonplace in building materials and furniture. Yet, people forget why these chemicals became popular in the first place.

They also forget about the terrible deaths and injuries caused by fires. Why do they forget? Because it doesn't happen as much anymore – in part because of the now widespread use of flame-retardants, which, within the last decade, has helped prevent house fires and fire-caused injuries.[124]

This forgetfulness partly accounts for why the alarmists have begun to call for the removal of flame-retardants from certain products and why moms seem utterly shocked that there are trace amounts of chemicals in little Johnny's superman zip-up pajamas.

But, the alarmists don't just want flame-retardants out of children's clothes, couches and building materials; they also want them removed from commercial airliners. Recent air disasters demonstrate the danger of this not-so-innocent request. When Asiana flight 214 crashed at San Francisco airport in the summer of 2013, all but three of the passengers were able to escape (the three young Chinese students who died where killed after being thrown from the plane and one of the girls was hit by a responding emergency vehicle after being coated in foam). While the plane did eventually catch fire and the roof was completely burned off, the flame-retardants used in the plane's walls, carpets and seats slowed the spread of the fire so that the flight crew could successfully extricate the passengers from the plane before it was engulfed.

Despite this convincing proof that these chemicals save lives, alarmists still want them removed from planes (and homes and pajamas and just about everything for which they're currently used). An article in *Scientific American* gets right to the alarmism when suggesting airline workers are exposed to more of the chemicals because of their time spent in the cabin:

> Spending about 100 hours each month in the air,
> flight attendants are bombarded with pesticides, ra-
> diation, ozone and any illnesses passengers carry on
> board. Now new research shows that they also fly
> along with some of the highest levels ever measured
> for some flame retardants.[125]

It isn't until the fourth paragraph that the author reveals that the
"health risks from the chemicals is unknown."[126] But you know what
is *known*? The health risks associated with plane crashes. In the
case of air disasters, the risk of death is high because planes—loaded with jet fuel—tend to burst into flames upon impact. Luckily, for
aircrews and passengers, planes are now manufactured with flame-
retardants, which, if the crash isn't catastrophic, can slow the progress of the fire. If the alarmists have their way, every crash would be
catastrophic, thanks to the removal of life-saving chemicals.

Chemicals have a bad reputation with many Americans, but
that's because we often forget that they were created to solve
problems for us. Once that problem is solved, one tends to forget
about it, but that doesn't mean the problem wouldn't come back if
we were to abandon the solutions. Consider another chemical in the
alarmists' crosshairs, the rather hard to pronounce phthalate (silent
"ph"), which is used to make plastics soft and malleable (think rubber ducky). Alarmists hyperventilate that this chemical is even present in children's toys—especially the ones that might make their way
into little junior's mouth (How could this be! How could a child's toy
contain a toxic chemical! I need a tissue!). While screaming about
the chemical, they fail to tell parents that without this chemical, Junior's nice, innocent, fun-to-chew-on rubber ducky becomes brittle,
hard, easily-broken-in-Johnny's-mouth rubber ducky.

What moms need to measure is the risk associated with a product that has trace levels of chemicals (levels which are nearly undetectable in human blood and which makes the product safer for baby to gum and squeeze and slam on the floor) against a the risk of allowing a child to gnaw on a chemical-free product (which might break more easily). If moms were informed of the consequences of the chemical-free choice (cuts to baby's mouth, swallowing shards of plastic, choking, etc.) rather than just fed hype about phthalates, parents might be be less inclined to get on board with the alarmists.

Alarmism about today's modern products—weather it's convenient, prepackaged, frozen and canned food, supposedly unsafe playground equipment, or chemicals in children's toys—must be taken with a grain of salt. Alarmists might sound like well-meaning, concerned public health and environmental activists, but parents should understand that they will be sacrificing some of the conveniences of modern life and may be making things less safe.

These activists paint a picture of Americans returning to a more agrarian lifestyle where people grow their own food or purchase it locally, raise animals (when possible) and rely on a much simpler (read: harder) lifestyle. Yet, in demanding this return to a simpler life, many betray their ignorance of history and the huge strides we have made in terms of health and safety—strides made, in part, because of the innovations in processing and the development of chemicals and other preservatives that the alarmists demonize.

CHAPTER 9

THE HIGH COSTS TO BUSINESSES AND JOBS

Each day, I try to pick up after my kids. I gather up the toys, put a few things in their proper place, and sweep up the crumbs left after the many meals and snacks eaten at the small kitchen table. I'm not quite sure why I put myself through this routine. Not 15 minutes after I've tidied up, I watch as the kids slowly repopulate the house with their toys, books and stuffed animals. It doesn't take long for my house to once again resemble the Titanic debris field.

I just shrug (and open a bottle of wine) and do it all again the next day.

Doing things for no reason is my own personal hang-up, yet increasingly alarmists are demanding businesses engage in the same type of dance, making gestures that have little effect other than to eat up their own time and resources.

This is no laughing matter: These unnecessary hoops created by alarmists and their government allies impact our economy. Companies spending more time and money on unnecessary changes to manufacturing means fewer productive jobs, higher prices for consumers, a shrinking private sector, and a turning back the clock on progress. And as too many families know too well, our struggling economy is a real cause for alarm.

Businesses naturally need to respond to the demands of their customers—that's generally how one runs a successful business and makes money—but the problem is that many of these businesses mistake radical activist groups as their average consumer. That just isn't the case. These organizations represent the fringe, the nervous alarmists who want greater restrictions on American commerce and less freedom for consumers to choose what to purchase. Acquiescing to the demands of these extremist groups typically means turning their backs on their real customer base, as well as rejecting sound science, product safety, and technological advancement.

A good example of this dynamic is the alarmists' push for companies to remove chemicals from their products—chemicals that actually keep these products safer for consumers. One such chemical (called parabens) is a preservative so common that today it's found in 80 percent of cosmetics and personal care products.

Manufacturers don't use parabens just to freak out hippy activists. They serve an important role in keeping products free from bacteria that can harm people (it's odd that the alarmists always seem to gloss over the real scary stuff, like bacteria that can cause serious illness and death).

Dermatologists also confirm the importance of parabens, saying they are necessary to keep products that require a shelf life (like makeup and moisturizers) safe and bacteria-free.[127] And according to New York City dermatologist Fran E. Cook-Bolden, "Parabens have a long history of safe use, and that's why they're commonplace. New preservatives have less of a proven track record."[128] I, for one, would rather continue to have my young children use products that have been used a long time without doing harm than moving unnecessarily to a new substance without that "proven track record" of safety. Wouldn't you? Indeed, parabens have been used in common food packaging, pharmaceuticals, cosmetics and personal care products for over 70 years. Let that factoid sink in for a little bit; Parabens aren't just some new fangled preservative, it's been around since the 50's!

If that doesn't reassure you how about this: Parabens have been tested and found to be safe by the FDA as well as any other international health agencies.[129] In fact, in May 2013, the European Commission's Scientific Committee on Consumer Safety issued a new report on parabens finding that they do not pose any health risk in the amounts currently used.[130] Even the American Cancer Society took the unusual step of pushing back on the alarmist claim that use of cosmetics and antiperspirants (which contain parabens) increase an individual's risk of developing breast cancer, saying in a statement: "There are no strong epidemiologic studies in the medical literature that link breast cancer risk and antiperspirant use, and very little scientific evidence to support this claim."[131]

It's certainly nice to have this official reassurance, yet, it is also important to remember that manufacturers also perform rigorous safety tests on their products. Sure, we can all give into the conspiracy theories that big business is out to kill us all, but from a practical standpoint, how do these companies benefit from killing off their own customers? And remember the big picture that as chemical use has increased, cancer rates have declined.[132] So much for that "more chemicals equals more cancer" line of reasoning.

Despite this reassurance (and even warnings about the consequences of removing parabens), some companies, such as high-end cosmetic giant Aveda, announced that they would comply with the demands of the scaredy-cats by pulling some of their products that contained parabens. The company even admitted the silliness of pulling these products in a statement:

> "Despite the fact that third-party review has confirmed that parabens of the type and concentration used by Aveda are safe, out of respect for consumer preference, we made the decision to reformulate products containing paraben-based preservatives..."[133]

Out of respect for consumer preference? Really? Was it the company's respect for consumers or the radical anti-chemical activists? And what of the millions of customers who didn't ask for the change but will certainly pay for the costs of the products' redesign?

So, just how successful was this campaign by alarmists to demand Aveda remove parabens from their products? Today Aveda's entire product line is paraben-free.[134] Soon, other companies followed suit. In 2012, another personal care product giant, Johnson and Johnson, announced plans to remove a number of chemicals, including parabens, from its line of consumer products by the end of 2015. A company executive explained the complexity (and implied cost) of removing these chemicals, saying:[135]

> Ms. Nettesheim [Johnson and Johnson vice president for product stewardship and toxicology for the

company's consumer health brands] said the project was a major undertaking and would require extensive spending on research and development to find suitable alternatives to the ingredients, most of which are common in the industry. She said new suppliers needed to be located and vetted, and testing was needed to ensure the replacements were also safe. The company declined to say how much the project would cost.

Then there's the delicate task of tinkering with products that have been popular for generations. The company's baby shampoo, for example, has been marketed for more than 50 years.

"Consumer acceptance is really important," Ms. Nettesheim said. "It really doesn't help you if you reformulate products and people don't like it."[136]

This means that one of America's largest companies is pouring resources into reformulating a product that is already perfectly safe and well regarded. Johnson and Johnson could have been investing in researching new products, expanding the company to new regions of the country and worldwide, cutting prices on their products, or creating jobs rather than following the marching order of alarmists.

Clearly, replacement preservatives can be found. In fact, other chemicals like germal, caprylyl glycol, and phenoxyethanol can be used in place of parabans. I'm glad these companies have found acceptable replacements, but how long until the chemical alarmists start sounding the alarm on these harmless additives?

Demands to omit chemicals isn't the only cost companies are absorbing thanks to the alarmists. Food products and restaurants are also struggling with the many demands of the food nannies and obesity scolds. While Mayor Bloomberg's soda-size restriction might naturally come to mind as the most notable of the food nanny initiatives, numerous other food-related restrictions are also making it tough and expensive for businesses to serve their customers.

Consider the menu labeling regulations (I discussed the junk science behind menu labeling efforts in Chapter 2) inserted into ObamaCare. The provision requires chain restaurants with 19 or more locations to provide calorie information on their menus and menu boards.

Estimates are that implementing the law will cost private businesses as much as $315.1 million.[137] Patrick Doyle, President and CEO of Dominos Pizza, captured the panic of many business owners when he chastised the Obama Administration in an opinion editorial for failing to understand the basics of how to run a business and how regulations like menu labeling not only kill innovation (in pizza toppings offered) but cost his company's individual franchisees tremendous profit loss:

> First, the FDA fails to account for the ways in which businesses actually service their customers. The proposed regulations would require our franchises to provide calorie information on in-store menu boards, a mandate which would cost each store thousands of dollars every year (starting at $1,600 and going up to $4,700 per year). As a delivery-oriented business, 90 percent of orders are placed by phone and online. As a result, the vast majority of our customers never even step foot in a store, much less look at the menu board. Incidentally, in New York and in other munici-

palities where we have already been forced to menu label, we have seen no change in customer ordering behavior. Unfortunately, the FDA's regulations are indifferent to these facts, and could result in millions of dollars of annual expenditures that a fraction of consumers actually see.[138]

These businesses will be paying more for these useless mandates, which mean that you'll be paying more too. And restaurants aren't the only businesses straining under this type of regulations.

Because grocery stores increasingly offer prepared meals and ready-to-eat dishes, chances are these businesses will also get twisted up in this burdensome regulatory net and be required to post calorie information near these products. If this happens, grocery stores, which already operate on a very thin margin, could incur costs upwards of $1 billion in the first year alone.[139] But it isn't just compliance costs these businesses have to consider. The bigger killer to their bottom line will be the legal costs if they fail to display the correct calorie information, which is likely to happen from time to time.

Let me explain how easily this could happen. To comply with the law, restaurants will send each menu item to a lab to be analyzed. That means, they'll produce one meal, box it up and send it off. Based on this analysis, restaurants will label their food. But think about it: Not every meal the cook prepares will end up looking or tasting the same. These dishes may not even contain the same rations of ingredients.

Consider the meals served at a Mexican restaurant: portions may vary from order to order, cooks have differing styles, some may have a heavy hand with the guacamole and cheese (high calorie) while others might load the burrito up with lettuce and pico de gallo (lower calorie). It's guaranteed that some changes will occur from one order to another. After all, these restaurants aren't run or staffed by robots (yes, that's the goal of the alarmists, but we're not there yet).

So, what will happen if there's variation in the calorie information for any given dish? The *New York Times* reported on this exact scenario in 2010, which provides a window into the challenge of keeping dishes to their labeled calorie counts:

> Some of the disparities were startling. At Denny's, a serving of grits, listed at 80 calories, tested at 258. The label on Lean Cuisine's shrimp and angel-hair pasta says it has 220 calories, but the researchers measured it at 319. They found 344 calories in a Wendy's grilled chicken wrap listed at 260.
>
> Misstatements went the other way, too. Fifteen of the samples had fewer calories than the stated amount. Denny's dry English muffin, for example contained 6 percent fewer calories than listed on the menu. A slice of Domino's thin-crust cheese pizza, listed at 180 calories, actually contained only 141.[140]

One can almost hear the trial lawyers' mouths watering at the very thought of this miscarriage of justice! Thanks to this menu labeling provision in ObamaCare, it looks like restaurants will lose what little profits are left to lawyers, consumers can count on less variation on menus (because what restaurant owner would change the menu if the new dish is required to be sent out to a lab for analysis?), higher prices (as customers pay for the cost to analyze food and label menus), and fewer choices (as many businesses close in the face of these and other government regulations). And of course, there's that little detail that menu labeling does exactly nothing to help people make healthier choices (covered in more detail in Chapter 2).

In New York City, restaurant owners have also had to focus on complying with Mayor Michael Bloomberg's ban on drinks larger than 16-ounces. While the ban has since been struck down by two New York City appeals court judges, the Mayor has vowed to fight on and other cities are expected to introduce similar restrictions. What do restaurant owners have to look forward to when similar city ordinances are passed? One New York restaurant owner described the headache of compliance and noted that he would lose at least $500 a week in profits.[141]

Unfortunately, meddling in private business has become a regular occurrence for government officials at all levels (are they bored?). Nor are the demands of the alarmists dying down.

In fact, the latest campaign by the alarmists calls for the ten largest retailers (big stores like Wal-Mart, Target, Walgreens, CVS) to pull products from store shelves if those products contain, in any amount, a list of 100 chemicals (like preservatives and flame-retardants). Because most products contain at least some trace amounts of chemicals in order to make them safer and give them a longer shelf life, compliance with this absurd campaign would mean stores would be forced to pull almost all of the products from their shelves. Kind of reminds me of the Soviet Union: long lines and nearly nothing on the grocery stores shelves. In the case of the Soviet Union, it was the government's strong control over the marketplace that led to product shortages. Today, it might very well be unnecessary fear.

Do you want to live that way? Do moms want to resort to less safe and effective products because of unfounded fears of perfectly safe products? Do consumers want businesses to give into the alarmists and change their products, making them more expensive, less safe, and less effective? Giving into the alarmists' demands will mean just that.

Instead, I say have courage. Speak up and let businesses know that you matter too. They have costumers—real costumers who spend their money in their stores for their products—who want the best they have to offer, not just what the alarmists will allow.

PART IV

························

HOW TO RECOGNIZE AND FIGHT BACK AGAINST ALARMISM

Keep Calm and Carry On
—British Government, 1939

Chapter 10

Fighting Fear

"Nothing in life is to be feared,
it is only to be understood."
— Marie Curie[142]

. . . .

I don't know about you, but I find being a mother difficult at times. Yes, incredible joy comes with being a mother but c'mon...it's hardly a nonstop party.

The dressing, diaper changing, getting through that seemingly endless basket of laundry, the water/milk/juice-providing, meal making and remaking, the cleaning, sweeping, mopping, scrubbing...and scrubbing, the negotiations and punishments, the praising, the yelling, the popsicle and cookie procuring, the wiping with a tissue (who am I kidding...wiping with my own sleeve), the worrying, fretting, hand wringing: It can all be wearying. Yet the alarmists want to add more tasks and worries to your already extensive list while taking away the very products, food, and activities that make being a parent (and a kid!) fun.

Alarmism brings with it not just uncertainty about the products we use, it makes parents uncertain about their own parenting skills. But that's the point. Alarmists love regulations and meddling and government minders running around tsk-tsk-ing (and if possible, stopping) the behaviors of others. They love to judge, shake their heads in disapproval, and make moms feel guilty. They want to plant the seed of doubt in people's minds so that parents more readily submit to government interference. Alarmists want obedience, and they know fear breeds just that.

I've fallen victim to alarmism myself. I've doubted my instincts after seeing some scary headline. I've paused to think back on the very few times I had a glass of wine while pregnant. I've let myself worry that maybe I shouldn't have allowed myself that that daily cup of fully caffeinated coffee. I've beat myself up for letting my kids watch a cartoon now and then, or for too often giving into their calls for a non-nutritious snack.

Then I snap out of it. I remember that I have enough real things to worry about and don't need the make believe.

I'm not the only one who is torn between these two worlds. A 2013 poll conducted by the Independent Women's Forum showed that the more women pay attention to these media-hyped health and safety concerns, the more they yearn for more warnings.[143]

Yet the same poll showed an overwhelming majority (83%) of women say they have difficulty discerning between legitimate concerns and scary headlines designed to attract attention. This means that women simply don't trust what they're being told, yet they're scared anyway and are desperate for more real information.

That's why it's important for women to fight back against the alarmists and their scaremongering tactics. Women want reliable information, not the dodgy science promoted by the alarmists and passed on by a compliant mainstream press. Women have choices in the marketplace right now. They don't need government minders and activist groups to tell them how to live or how to raise their children.

Here are some easy steps to fight back against the alarmists:

1) TUNE OUT AND TURN OFF

Whoa...hold on. I'm not suggesting you become a hermit, toss the television, drop your Internet service and throw away your computer and mobile devices. No one is suggesting you go dark. But it's important to keep a healthy attitude toward information and some distance from the worst alarmists.

All of us are lucky to live in an age of such cutting edge technological advances. We should celebrate the vast number of resources out there to gather information. But information can overwhelm and nurture alarmism. This is sometimes referred to as "information via fire hose" where the information comes at you at so quickly that it overwhelms, leaving you drenched but confused.

That's why it's important to realize that not all information is useful and much of it is misleading if not downright false. Alarmists understand that many parents are too busy to fact check the latest scary news story. They prey on these too-busy moms telling them they should just operate on the "better safe than sorry" theory— meaning they should change their habits no matter if the claim is true or not.

Limiting your time online is one way to reduce the effectiveness of the alarmists because it simply robs them of the avenue by which they reach parents. I'm guilty of failing to unplug myself. On a recent vacation, my husband and I rarely went offline. We used our mobile devices to check restaurant reviews, take pictures, check the weather, get directions, read the history of certain locations we visited and even watch an old movie on Netflix in the hotel room after the kids went to sleep. I think these technologies enhanced, rather than detracted from our experience. But I did take care not to check out the news sites or parenting blogs. I know that when it comes to the latest scary headline, you simply have to limit your time online.

2) Become a Skeptic

Alarmists are variation of conspiracy theorists. They operate in the same way. Sure, the alarmists I've written about in this book don't generally associate with the Birther movement (Obama was born in Kenya) or the creepy Truther types (9/11 was an inside job). I doubt the alarmists see themselves as allies of Area 51 theorists (aliens are among us) or the now-retro two shooter blue hairs (JFK's assassination). But make no mistake, these two groups are close cousins.

The alarmist conspiracy of choice revolves around big bad corporations. They promote the idea that large corporations are out to get us, seek to control us, and if possible, kill us. Consider comments by well-known food nanny Michelle Simon who let her truly crazy side show when she said: "Thanks to the right wing, we have deregulated every single aspect of corporate behavior, so that killing people is perfectly legal."[144]

It's important to remember that corporations only exist if people continue to buy their products and services. They have to focus on providing what we need or they will go out of business.

This doesn't mean that the business world is made up of angels. Far from it. In fact, corporations do make mistakes and behave badly (anyone remember Enron?). Corporations do break the law, cost taxpayers billions in bailouts, influence the marketplace by lobbying for waivers and protections not afforded to small businesses, and can generally harm consumers by shutting down competition.

But the utter vilification—the almost cartoon like characterization of corporations—is where the alarmists go too far.

That's why some skepticism is necessary. Alarmist organizations want you to believe they are the good guys (along with government regulators, public health officials and other food and products nannies), and the corporations are the bad guys. This just isn't true.

Alarmists don't like to admit it, but corporations aren't the only ones driven by money. For instance, scientists often rely on government grants to further their research goals. This reliance betrays the reason why scientific studies (of all quality) often conclude with the familiar line "more research is required." That's code for "please send more money!"

Alarmist organizations, like the Center for Science in the Public Interest, profit from newsletter subscriptions. The CSPI's own website claims 2 million people read its newsletters. At $20 for a year's subscription, that means CSPI brings in $40 million just from subscription payments. But the marketers at CSPI aren't dumb. They know bad news sells a whole lot more subscriptions than stories about cancer rates coming down (which is the truth). For CSPI, alarmism pays handsomely.

Lastly, government officials use alarmism to expand their power and their very existence. After all, fear makes them necessary. Government officials and alarmist organizations work well together. The officials cite the junk science promoted by the organizations, and the organizations suggest the government official is the only one who can solve the problems they research. It's a match made in regulatory hell.

So, when you hear claims that something is dangerous, do as a skeptic would do: Inject a little doubt into the debate. Ask questions. Demand facts. Read the research. Be your own best advocate. But, for heaven's sake, don't just believe the alarmists.

3) Beware the Mommy Blogs

Mommy blogs have their place. They're great for tips on crafts, where to go on a rainy day, fool-proof, kid friendly recipes, as well as helpful advice on clothing and footwear. But, be warned, something increasingly smells rotten in the mommy blogosphere.

Hmmm...how shall I say this nicely? Many lady bloggers can be more than a tiny bit sanctimonious and promote the alarmist narrative. Yup...that's right, your friendly, funny, self-deprecating mommy blogger might just be in cahoots with the alarmists to make your life a whole lot more difficult.

Consider the subtle yet more frequent messages woven into many of these popular blogs. A recipe for strawberry jam might include the word "organic" before the fruit in the ingredient list. The blogger might suggest you use local berries (preferably picked yourself) or maybe the recipe will offer advice on how you can switch out "all-natural" agave nectar instead of using "toxic, scary, awful" sugar (I always chuckle when I see this suggestion that sugar isn't natural). Replete with gorgeous photography, many of these blogs demand you do more, with less, better, faster, and cleaner!

These might seem like minor suggestions, but they carry a big message. They subtly pass judgment on those who purchase conventional food or who rely on canned, frozen or the occasional convenience food item.

Mommy blogs are also quite adept at passing on unfounded fears of chemicals. A popular mommy blog called Momsrising (doesn't that sound nice like we're all rising like the phoenix or that we're rising to the occasion?) claims to be a place "Where moms and people who love them go to change our world."[145] But the change they seek is quite frightening. They pass on the junkiest of junk science, scare the wits out of families and tell moms they should push for greater regulations on the manufacturing and retail sectors. Yet despite the nonsense they preach (one of their more recent claims is that toxins are hiding in Windex and other cleaners... uh, yeah, but no one's drinking Windex so calm down!), Momsrising is known for their "stroller brigades" of moms who want common, everyday products taken away from consumers.

What women need to understand is that moms aren't all made from the same mold. We don't all live in the tony neighborhood of Park Slope, Brentwood, or Cleveland Heights. We don't all have the money to buy the expensive niche-brand products, organic food, and pricy farmers market produce. Women must recognize this diversity and encourage their fellow moms to do the best they can by feeding their children healthy food at the prices that match their own budgets. The food snobs might turn their nose up at canned or frozen food but getting fruits and vegetables this way is just as healthy as eating fresh produce (some studies say canned and frozen are even more nutritious than fresh!). No one should insist parents only shop at high-end grocery stores. Instead, parents should be encouraged to buy healthier items from whatever store is closest, most convenient, and offers the best prices for their family's budget. Demonizing other people's food choices is the great danger of alarmism—it makes moms feel guilty about their perfectly healthy and appropriate choices.

4) *NOT EVERYONE LIVES AT DOWNTON ABBEY; PROGRESS IS YOUR FRIEND*

The alarmists have a habit of romanticizing the past. They grieve the good 'ole days when everyone grew her own produce and raised a nice, manageable assortment of animals on a small plot of land from which milk and meat could help feed the family.

In the alarmists' perfect world, we'd all have to make seven different stops to do the grocery shopping (the dairy, the butcher, the farm stand for vegetables, the drug store for medicines, the five and dime for paper products, etc.). They moon over the days when humans used wooden bowls and carried water in ostrich eggshells. At night, they'd suggest we all sit around a fire and tell stories or perhaps walk to the local watering hole for a pint of ale. It's all very Hobbiton, and it certainly is nice to read about in stories. But it's a Tolkien nightmare when applied to the modern world.

What the alarmists leave out of these sentimental tales of days gone by is that if you lived the "simple" way as we did hundreds of years ago, you'd probably die before your thirtieth birthday—particularly women who bore the strain of having children. You'd better hope you don't hurt yourself, because you won't have access to modern medicine. Since birth control pills and condoms contain chemicals, you'll simply have to accept having a large family. Maybe that's okay, because with all the acreage to till and animals to tend, you'll need the extra help. Of course, without vaccinations, several of those kids will die of diseases that are preventable today, like diphtheria, measles, mumps, scarlet fever, whooping cough, and polio. Without advances in agriculture, like the continued use of GMOs, pesticides, and herbicides, food will become extremely hard to produce and sustain, which means the surviving children will likely die of starvation.

This might sound like a wild exaggeration, but modern parents have no understanding of just how common childhood deaths were as recently as 100 years ago. I often think about the fragility of life when I look back on a very scary incident involving my middle child who developed a small sore on his stomach. I put some over-the-counter antibiotic cream on the spot, but it kept getting worse. The sore swelled, started bleeding and oozing puss, and he developed a fever. I took him to the doctor and was told he had a Methicillin-Resistant Staphylococcus Aureus infection, more commonly known by its acronym—MRSA.

The doctors were rather nonchalant about the whole thing, explaining that my husband and I would have to drain the now-much larger wound daily (this alone was heartbreaking to watch as the pain was so severe), wipe down the entire house with a bleach and water solution, and give him antibiotics for about 10 days.

The medication worked and my son recovered, but it made an impression on me. What would have happened without those antibiotics and powerful germ killers? Would the infection have gotten worse and spread to my other sons, or to my husband and me? While MRSA is a modern disease, generations of parents were forced to watch their children suffer similar painful infections and die of diseases without the aid of these modern innovations.

So, when you hear an alarmist talking about returning to a "simpler" time or a more agrarian way of living, put it into perspective. Remember how lucky we are to live with modern conveniences, a robust agriculture sector that is able to feed our nation as well as much of the rest of the world, modern manufacturing that produces safe products free of bacteria, and advanced medical care.

5) DIVERSIFY YOUR SOURCES

Alarmism is tough to miss. It's everywhere! One moment you're watching a Today Show segment featuring some celebrity chef offer tips on perfect fried chicken and then *bam*, the show switches to a nail biter on how your e-reader and smart phone is made with "toxic" heavy metals (calm down, they're not toxic unless you eat your e-reader and smart phone).

So, if you happen to see one of these reports or read one of the many stories out there claiming that you're being poisoned by the things in your purse, try finding an alternative voice. Simply Google-ing the latest drama might do the trick.

For instance, a friend of mine recently posted a story on Face-book about the German government's plans to shutter the entire country's nuclear power plants in favor of "wind and other sustain-able forms of energy." The article made me curious because I knew these sustainable energy sources couldn't match the power output produced by nuclear energy. So, I did a little research on my own.

It didn't take much digging to discover that instead of replac-ing nuclear energy with wind, solar, and algae-power, the Germans were investing in the construction of 22 coal-burning plants. I have nothing against coal, but the claim that nuclear would be replaced entirely with these "environmentally friendly" energy sources was untrue. In fact, Germany wasn't moving toward cleaner energy, they were replacing one of the cleanest forms of energy (nuclear) with one of the most pollutive (coal). Congrats!

The bottom line: Do your own research. There are good writers out there doing important work to debunk the claims of the alarm-ists—from food to agriculture to energy and chemicals. Here are a few of my favorite writers on the various alarmist topics:

✦ On chemicals: **Trevor Butterworth** is editor-at-large for STATS.org, a non-profit research organization that exam-ines public policy and the media. Butterworth writes for Newsweek, The Daily Beast and is a columnist at Forbes.com. He has perhaps the best Twitter handle: @Butterwor-thy. **Angela Logomasini** writes at the Competitive Enter-prise Institute (CEI.org) and provides serious, yet easy to understand, analysis of the latest chemical alarmism. She can be followed on Twitter at @alogomasini.

✦ On Genetically Modified Organisms (GMOs): As a former news producer, **Jon Entine** understands how the media works. He's firmly nonpolitical, focusing on the science, not the politics of an issue. He written books on GMOs and runs a program called the Genetic Literacy Program at George Mason University, which promotes a better understanding of genetics and general science literacy. **Greg Conko**, author of *The Frankenfood Myth: How Protest and Politics Threaten the Biotech Revolution* is another must-read if you want to familiarize yourself with the alarmists' use of hard-to-understand biotechnology concepts as a weapon against the average consumer. See Greg's work at CEI.org. I also really enjoy reading **the scholars at Biofortified,** particularly Anastasia Bodnar and Karl Haro von Mogel. Firmly non-political, these writers are dedicated to facts, not political expediency. Check them out at Biofortified.org. Thankfully, the mainstream media is beginning to write fair pieces about GMOs. Check out Nathanael Johnson at Grist.org. The New York Times and Scientific American have come out in support of GMOs and regularly print thoughtful and well-researched pieces on the issue. Recently, both publications' editorial boards ran pieces in support of GMOs.

✦ On food: **Jayson Lusk**, author of a *The Food Police: A Well-Fed Manifesto About the Politics of Your Plate,* examines and debunks a number of the sacred cows of the anti-obesity alarmists. **J. Eric Oliver**'s book *Fat Politics: The Real Story Behind America's Obesity Epidemic* and **Paul Campos'** book *The Obesity Myth: Why America's Obsession with*

Weight Is Hazardous to Your Health are good resources to understanding alarmist efforts to hype the obesity issue. **Walter Olson** is a Cato scholar who also runs the popular legal blog Overlawyered.com. Olson focuses on tort reform and overregulation. **Baylen Linnekin** runs KeepFoodLegal. org where he often examines the constitutionality of food laws and promotes the right of Americans to grow, raise, produce, buy, sell, share, cook, eat, and drink the foods of their own choosing. And of course, be sure to visit the **Culture of Alarmism's webpage at CultureofAlarmism.org**, where writers (including yours truly) take on the alarmists, debunk their paper-thin claims, and offer reassurance to nervous parents.

✦ **The Independent Women's Forum** is also a good place to get perspective. Established over 20 years ago, IWF tackles another type of alarmism—the one that works to convince women they need special protections from the big, bad man-ruled world. www.iwf.org

✦ My favorite Mommy Blogger: You won't find prolific blogger, photographer, and newly-minted Food Network star Ree Drummond, popularly called **The Pioneer Woman**, telling you that you "simply must!" buy an organic chicken to make her recipe's work. Drummond has an almost psychic understanding of what busy moms need: good, nutritionally dense, kid-friendly, reasonably-priced, easy-to-make-on-a busy-night food. She leaves the lecturing to other food bloggers. (ThePioneerWoman.com)

✦ If you need to laugh at the alarmists, visit the always-entertaining **Chicks on the Right**. They don't get too deep into the science, but they do a great job of making fun of the food nannies and obesity scolds. (ChicksontheRight.com)

✦ There are a few good books out there that attempt to knock the wind out of the alarmists puffed up sails, but perhaps the most comprehensive take down is provided by **Matt Ridley's** *Rational Optimist* which offers a reasonable (and thoroughly witty) argument against the alarmists' doom and gloom.

✦ **Free-Range Kids** is another great site. Run by "the worst mom in the world" (a nickname she got because she let her 9 year old son ride on the subway alone), Lenore Skenazy works to fight back against claims that "our children are in constant danger from creeps, kidnapping, germs, grades, flashers, frustration, failure, baby snatchers, bugs, bullies, men, sleepovers and/or the perils of a non-organic grape." (FreeRangeKids.com)

✦ Guess what? Farmers run blogs too! And that's good for consumers who have lots of questions and now, thanks to the alarmists, more worries. So, go to the source. Worried about pesticides? See what Dairy Carrie has to say about why she sprays her fields: (DairyCarrie.com). Worried about animal cruelty? Check out what this mom and hog farmer has to say about why pigs are sometimes put in crates and how the meat industry is responding to consumer concerns. (MomattheMeatCounter.blogspot.com). Think "Big Ag" means bad farmers? This blogger's family farm is considered a "Big Ag" operation because the farm is a corporation. Check out Maria Bowers' thoughts on being demonized by the alarmists. (OregonGreen.wordpress.com)

6) *Trust Your Instincts and Don't Give Into the Alarmism*

It's easy to be pessimistic about the future. The American economy has been sputtering along for almost six years, fuel and food prices continue to rise, the threat of terrorism continues, and Americans see many, very basic freedoms slipping away. Yet, increasingly, Americans are being told not to focus on the large, fundamental problems facing our country, but to fear the everyday, common products and foods that make life easier and more enjoyable.

This book isn't supposed to be an ode to Bobby McFerrin's '80's classic to not worry and be happy, but it is a call to put things into perspective. People should know what they are eating and be informed if a product has proven harmful, but they should take the headlines with a grain of salt.

Trust your instincts as a parent. In general, people know what's good for them and their kids. They understand that carrots are better than candy and that a salad with grilled chicken is a better dinner choice than a burger and fries. Parents know they shouldn't let their kids eat plastic or spray cleaners or a full bottle of hand lotion. People need to remind their kids to chew, to be careful on the playground, and to eat their peas and carrots before dessert. Parents must parent and turn off the television. They need to cook simple meals for their families and start putting their children to bed at a reasonable hour. These are the simple and basic things that make families work.

Don't let the alarmists make it more complicated. Don't let them take the fun out of life or make you needlessly worry. You can take their power away by simply tuning them out.

That would be a nice change.

It may even make the alarmists a little alarmed themselves.

ENDNOTES

· ·

1   Ridley, Matt. *The Rational Optimist: How Prosperity Evolves*. New York: Harper, 2010. 280. Print.

2   Finch, Peter, perf. Network. Dir. Sidney Lumet. MGM, United Artists, 1976. Film.

3   Kravet, David, "iPhone Jailbreaking Could Crash Cellphone Towers, Apple Claims." *Wired.com*. Wired Magazine. Web. July 28, 2009.

4   "BPA in Kids' Canned Food." *Breastcancerfund.org*. Breast Cancer Fund. Web. n.a. September 2011.

5   Ibid.

6   U.S. Food and Drug Administration. "FDA Continues to Study BPA." *FDA. gov*. FDA. Web. March 30, 2012. Available at: http://www.fda.gov/ForConsumers/ConsumerUpdates/ucm297954.htm.

7   Teeguarden, Justin G., et al., "Twenty-Four Hour Human Urine and Serum Profiles of Bisphenol A during High-Dietary Exposure," *Toxicological Sciences*, 2011, 123 (1), pp. 48-57. Available at: http://toxsci.oxfordjournals.org/content/123/1/48.abstract

8   Butterworth, Trevor. "Science Suppressed: How America became obsessed with BPA." *Stats.org*. Statistical Assessment Service, George Mason University. Web, June 12, 2009.

9   "Kids' Soup Cans Contain BPA Toxins." *News.discovery.com*. Discovery News. N.a. Web. September 21, 2001. Available at: http://news.discovery.com/human/bpa-toxins-canned-food-110921.htm

10   Moisse, Katie. "BPA in Canned Foods: Should You Worry?" *abcnews.go.com*. ABC News. Web. Sept. 21, 2011.

11   Sager, Jeanne. "Your Kids Are Eating These Canned Foods Loaded With BPA." *Thestir.cafemom.com*. The Stir. Web. September 22, 2011.

12   "BPA found in canned Thanksgiving foods, Breast Cancer Fund reports." *Consumerreports.org*. Consumer Reports News. N.a. Web. November 15, 2011.

13   Entine, Jon. "Campbell's Big Fat Green BPA Lie -- and the Sustainability Activists who enabled It." *Forbes Online*. Forbes. Web. September 18, 2012. Available at: http://www.forbes.com/sites/jonentine/2012/09/18/campbells-big-fat-green-bpa-lie-and-the-sustainability-activists-that-enabled-it/2/

14   ibid.

15   Campbell's Soup Company. "Nourishing our Planet." *Campbellsoupcompany.com*. N.p., n.d. Web. Available at:
http://www.campbellsoupcompany.com/csr/planet_packaging.asp

16   Tavernise, Sabrina. "F.D.A. Makes It Official: BPA Can't Be Used in Baby Bottles and Cups" *NYTimes.com*. The New York Times. Web. July 17, 2012. Available at: http://www.nytimes.com/2012/07/18/science/fda-bans-bpa-from-baby-bottles-and-sippy-cups.html?_r=0

17   U.S. Food and Drug Administration. "Bisphenol A (BPA): Use in Food Contact Application." *FDA.gov*. N.a. March 2013. Available at: http://www.fda.gov/newsevents/publichealthfocus/ucm064437.htm

18   Seymour, Julia. "Media, Left Try to Put Their Hands on Your Shopping Cart." *MRC.org*. Media Research Center. Web. June 20, 2012. Available at: http://www.mrc.org/special-reports/media-left-try-put-their-hands-your-shopping-cart

19   Green, Dominic. "Here Are All The People Plotting To Kill The McDonald's Happy Meal." *BusinessInsider.com*. Business Insider. Web. April 25, 2013. Web. Available at: http://www.businessinsider.com/could-the-happy-meal-die-2013-4#ixzz2ePx8xbc7

20   Jaslow, Ryan. "Eating out? Beware of these Xtreme restaurant foods, watchdog warns." *CBSNews.com*. CBS News. Web. January 16, 2013. Available at: http://www.cbsnews.com/8301-204_162-57564370/eating-out-beware-of-these-xtreme-restaurant-foods-watchdog-warns/

21   Masterson, Kathryn. "Food cop: Love him or hate him." *Chicagotribune.com*. The Chicago Tribune. Web. October 4, 2007.

22   "5 Facts You Need to Know About Synthetic Artificial Food Coloring!" *Thesleuthjournal.com*. The Sleuth Journal. N.a. Web. November 4, 2012. Available at: http://www.thesleuthjournal.com/5-facts-you-need-to-know-about-synthetic-artificial-food-coloring/

23   Chasmar, Jessica. "Nonprofit likens sugary soda to a 'ruthlessly efficient bioweapon'." *Washingtontimes.com*. The Washington Times. Web. February

13, 2013. Available at: http://www.washingtontimes.com/news/2013/feb/18/nonprofit-likens-sugary-soda-ruthlessly-efficient-/

24   Ibid

25   Browning, Dominique. "Is Your Garden Hose Toxic?" *Ideas.Time.com*. Time Magazine. Web. August 2, 2012. Available at: http://ideas.time.com/2012/08/02/is-your-garden-hose-toxic/#ixzz2cFPOEkrQ

26   Moyer, Christine S. "Pediatricians' alert focuses on choking dangers." *Amednews.com*. American Medical News. Web. March 11, 2010. Available at: http://www.ama-assn.org/amednews/2010/03/08/prse0311.htm

27   American Academy of Pediatrics. "Policy Statement—Prevention of Choking Among Children." *AAPPublications.org*. Official Journal of the American Academy of Pediatrics. N.a Web. 2010. Available at: http://pediatrics.aappublications.org/content/early/2010/02/22/peds.2009-2862.abstract

28   Federal Interagency Forum on Child and Family Statistics. "POP1 Child population: Number of children (in millions) ages 0–17 in the United States by age, 1950–2012 and projected 2013–2050." *Childstats.org*. Federal Interagency Forum on Child and Family Statistics. Available at: http://www.childstats.gov/americaschildren/tables/pop1.asp?popup=true

29   Szabo, Liz. "Pediatricians call for a choke-proof hot dog." *USAToday.com*. USA Today. Web. February 22, 2010. Available at: http://usatoday30.usatoday.com/news/health/2010-02-22-1Achoke22_ST_N.htm

30   Ibid.

31   U.S. Centers for Disease Control and Prevention. "Falls: The Reality." *CDC.gov*. The Centers For Disease Control and Prevention, National Center for Injury Prevention and Control. April 12, 2012. Available at: http://www.cdc.gov/SafeChild/Falls/

32   Morran, Chris. "2,010 Calorie Cold Stone Shake Named Worst Drink In America." *Consumerist.com*. Consumerist. May 27, 2010. Available at: http://consumerist.com/2010/05/27/2010-calorie-cold-stone-shake-named-worst-drink-in-america/

33   Ibid.

34   "Bloomberg On Soda Ban: "We're Simply Forcing You To Understand."" *Realclearpolitics.com*. Real Clear Politics. N.a. May 31, 2012. Available at: http://www.realclearpolitics.com/video/2012/05/31/bloomberg_on_sad_ban_were_simply_forcing_you_to_understand.html

35   Chumley, Cheryl K. "NYC Mayor Bloomberg: Government has right to 'infringe on your freedom'." *Washingtontimes.com*. The Washington Times. Web. March 25, 2013. Available at: http://www.washingtontimes.com/news/2013/mar/25/nyc-mayor-bloomberg-government-has-right-infringe-/

36   Sunstein, Cass. "Super-Sized Americans Need the Choice of Fewer Fries." *Bloomberg.com*. Bloomberg View. Web. February 12, 2013.

37   "Eating Healthy: Whose Choice Should It Be?" *NPR.org*. National Public Radio, All Things Considered. Web. October 15, 2011. Available at: http://m.npr.org/news/Health/141383327

38   "100 Million Dieters, $20 Billion: The Weight-Loss Industry by the Numbers." *Abcnews.go.com*. ABC News, 20/20. New York, NY, n.a. Web. May 8, 2012.

Available at: http://abcnews.go.com/Health/100-million-dieters-20-billion-weight-loss-industry/story?id=16297197#.UcxZ053D_IU

39   "Nutrition Facts food labels are too confusing for most people, FDA re-searchers say." *NewYorkDailyNews.com*. New York Daily News. Web. Janu-ary 24, 2013. Available at: http://www.nydailynews.com/life-style/health/food-labels-confuse-people-fda-study-article-1.1246816

40   "Study: Fewer food choices don't help weight loss." *Foxnews.com*. Fox News. Web. June 1, 2012. http://www.foxnews.com/health/2012/06/01/study-fewer-food-choices-dont-help-weight-loss/#ixzz2Kn2Qlhk1

41   Cardello, Hank. "Lower-calorie foods and beverages dramatically boosted revenue at 16 food and beverage companies that account for nearly $100 billion in annual sales." *Hudson.org*. The Hudson Institute. Web. March 13,2013. http://www.hudson.org/

42   "More Americans reaching age 90 than ever before." *CBSNews.com*. CBS News. Web. November 17, 2011. http://www.cbsnews.com/8301-201_162-57326882/more-americans-reaching-age-90-than-ever-before/

43   Jemal, Ahmedin, et al. "Annual Report to the Nation on the Status of Cancer, 1975-2009, Featuring the Burden and Trends in HPV-Associated Cancers and HPV Vaccination Coverage Levels." *Seer.cancer.gov*. U.S. National Insti-tutes of Health, National Cancer Institute. Web. October 19, 2012. Available at: http://seer.cancer.gov/report_to_nation/

44   Centers for Disease Control and Prevention. NCHS Data Brief, "Death in the United States, 2010." *CDC.gov*. Centers for Disease Control and Prevention, National Center for Health Statistics. Web. July 27, 2012. Available at: http://www.cdc.gov/nchs/data/databriefs/db99.htm

45   Hellmich, Nanci. "Death rate down, life expectancy up in U.S." *USAToday30. usatoday.com*. USA Today. Web. March 17, 2011. Available at: http://usato-day30.usatoday.com/news/health/story/2011/03/Death-rate-down-life-ex-pectancy-up-in-US/44935852/1

46   Murray, Christopher J. L., MD, DPhil, et al. "The State of US Health, 1990-2010 Burden of Diseases, Injuries, and Risk Factors." *jama.jamanetwork.com*. The Journal of the American Medical Association. Vol. 310, No. 6. Web. August 14, 2013. Web.

47   Reuell, Peter. "Good health lasts later in life." *News.harvard.edu*. Harvard Ga-zette. Web. July 30, 2013.
Available at: http://news.harvard.edu/gazette/story/2013/07/good-health-longer/

48   Sagan, Carl. "Encyclopaedia Galactica." *Cosmos: A Personal Voyage*. Epi-sode 12. 01:24. PBS. December 14, 1980.

49   Safe Fruits and Veggies. *Safefruitsandveggies.com*. n.p. n.d. Web. Available at: http://www.safefruitsandveggies.com/sites/default/files/pesticides-in-perspective.pdf

50   Davis, Geoff, "5 Tips for Buying Earth-Friendly Wood Furniture and Lum-ber." *Giamlife.com*. Web. n.d. Available at: http://life.gaiam.com/article/5-tips-buying-earth-friendly-wood-furniture-and-lumber

51   Lorentzen, Ronald. Weblog comment. *Nature.com*. Nature 464, 1103 - 1104 (7292) Web. August 12, 2010.

52   Solnick, Sara J. and Hemenway, David. "The 'Twinkie Defense': the relationship between carbonated non-diet soft drinks and violence perpetration among Boston high school students." *injuryprevention.bmj.com*. Injury Prevention. Web. October 24, 2011.

53   Ibid.

54   The Breast Cancer Fund. "BPA in Kids' Canned Food." *Breastcancerfund.org*. The Breast Cancer Fund. September 2011. Available at: http://www.breastcancerfund.org/big-picture-solutions/make-our-products-safe/cans-not-cancer/bpa-in-kids-canned-food.html

55   Goodson, WH 3rd et al. "Activation of the mTOR pathway by low levels of xenoestrogens in breast epithelial cells from high-risk women." *Carcin.oxfordjournals.org*. Oxford Journals: Carcinogenesis. Available at: http://carcin.oxfordjournals.org/content/32/11/1724

56   Janabi, Fourat. "Not All Scientific Statements Have Equal Weight." *Random Rationality: Biting off more than I can chew*. n.d. Available at: http://randomrationality.com/2013/06/03/not-all-scientific-statements-have-equal-weight/

57   Butterworth, Trevor. "Can Plastic Change Your Sex?" *Forbes.com*. Forbes. Web. November 19, 2009.

58   Barnes, Melody. "White House Task Force on Childhood Obesity" *Letsmove.gov*. Let's Move. Print. May 2010. Available at: http://www.letsmove.gov/sites/letsmove.gov/files/TaskForce_on_Childhood_Obesity_May2010_FullReport.pdf

59   Wisdom, J., Downs, J.S., Loewenstein, G. "Promoting Healthy Choices: Information versus Convenience." American Economic Journal: Applied Economics, 2, 2010. 164–178.

60   Barnes, Melody. "White House Task Force on Childhood Obesity" *Letsmove.gov*. Let's Move. May 2010. Available at: http://www.letsmove.gov/sites/letsmove.gov/files/TaskForce_on_Childhood_Obesity_May2010_FullReport.pdf

61   Elbel, Brian, et al. "Calorie Labeling And Food Choices: A First Look At The Effects On Low-Income People In New York City." *Healthaffairs.org*. Health Affairs, November/December 2009 vol. 28 no. 6 w1110-w1121. Web. October 2009. Available at: http://content.healthaffairs.org/content/28/6/w1110.full

62   Ibid.

63   Ibid.

64   Roan, Sheri, "Menu labeling law doesn't register a blip at Taco Time." *Articles.latimes.com*. The Los Angeles Times. Web. January 14, 2011.

65   Elbel, B., et al. "Child and adolescent fast-food choice and the influence of calorie labeling: a natural experiment." *Nature.com/ijo*. International Journal of Obesity (2011) 35, 493–500. Web. February 15, 2011. Available at: http://www.nature.com/ijo/journal/v35/n4/abs/ijo20114a.html

66 Carnegie Mellon University. "Press Release: Recommended Calorie Information on Menus Does Not Improve Consumer Choices, Carnegie Mellon Study Shows." *CMU.edu*. Carnegie Mellon News. N.a., Web. July 18, 2013.

67 Ibid.

68 "Simpler Lifestyle Found to Reduce Exposure to Endocrine Disrupting Chemicals." *Sciencedaily.com*. Science Daily. N.a. Web. June 26, 2012. Available at: http://www.sciencedaily.com/releases/2012/06/120626092546.htm

69 Ibid.

70 Ibid.

71 Williams, Forence, "Eat Like a Mennonite." *NYTimes.com*. New York Times. Web. January 18, 2013. Available at:
http://www.nytimes.com/2013/01/19/opinion/eat-like-a-mennonite.html?_r=0

72 Mann, Denise. "Simple lifestyle may limit exposure to chemicals." *Women.webmd.com*. WebMD. Web. June 26, 2012. Available at: http://women.webmd.com/news/20120626/simple-lifestyle-may-limit-exposure-to-chemicals

73 Fisher KA, Newbold KB, Eyles JD, Elliott SJ. "Physical health in a Canadian Old Order Mennonite community." *Rural and Remote Health* 13: 2252. Web. March 28, 2013. Available: http://www.rrh.org.au

74 Tribe, David. "600+ Published Safety Assessments." Web log post. *GMO-Pundit.blogspot.com*. n.d. Web. Available at: http://gmopundit.blogspot.com/p/450-published-safety-assessments.html

75 Koerner, Brendan. "How Much of Our Food Is Bioengineered?" *Slate.com*. Slate. Web. May 22, 2003.

76 Biology Fortified. Studies with Independent Funding. *Biofortified.org*. Web. n.d. Available at: http://www.biofortified.org/genera/studies-for-genera/independent-funding/

77 Snell, Chelsea, et al. "Assessment of the health impact of GM plant diets in long-term and multigenerational animal feeding trials: A literature review." *Food and Chemical Toxicology*. Volume 50. Issues 3-4. March – April 2012. Pages 1134 – 1148. Web. Available at: http://www.sciencedirect.com/science/article/pii/S0278691511006399

78 "GMOs: are there any risks? Launch of a European Round Table on GMO Safety." Brussels. European Union. N.a. October 8, 2001. Web. Available here: http://ec.europa.eu/research/press/2001/pr0810en.html

79 Busquin, Phillippe. "EC-Sponsored Research on Safety of Genetically Modified Organisms, A Review of Results." *Ec.europa.eu*. European Commission. n.d. Web. Available at: http://ec.europa.eu/research/quality-of-life/gmo/

80 Vaughan, Adam. "French ban of Monsanto GM maize rejected by EU." *theguardian.com*. The Guardian. Web. May 22, 2012.

81 "French study finds tumours in rats fed GM corn." *Reuters.com*. Thomas Reuters. Web. September 19, 2012. Available at: http://www.reuters.com/article/2012/09/19/gmcrops-safety-idUSL5E8KJAGN20120919

82 Ibid.

83 Moreno, Andy. "GMO Effects on Tumor Growth with Gilles-Eric Séralini, Ph.D." Online video clip. *YouTube*. YouTube. October 20, 2012. Available at: http://youtu.be/Zbtj2_EtF5E

84 Genetically Modified Food, Pt. 1. Doctoroz.com. The Doctor Oz Show. N.a. n.d. Available at: http://www.doctoroz.com/videos/genetically-modified-foods-pt-1

85 Weber, Jack Adam. "Anti-GMO Victory — Kenya to ban all imports of GMO foods." *Str8talkchronicles.com*. Web. December 12, 2012. Available at: http://str8talkchronicles.com/?p=28748

86 World Food Program. "Mobile Cash For Emergency Response In Kenya." *Wfp.org*. World Food Program. Web. N.a. n.d. Available at: http://www.wfp.org/countries/kenya

87 MacKenzie, Debora. "Study linking GM crops and cancer questioned." *Newscientist.com*. Web. September 19, 2012. Available at: http://www.newscientist.com/article/dn22287-study-linking-gm-crops-and-cancer-questioned.html?DCMP=OTC-rss&nsref=online-news#.UfPh9p3D_IU

88 Revkin, Andrew C. "Six French Science Academies Dismiss Study Finding GM Corn Harmed Rats." *Nytimes.com*. The New York Times. Web. October 19, 2012. Available at: http://dotearth.blogs.nytimes.com/2012/10/19/six-french-science-academies-dismiss-study-finding-gm-corn-harmed-rats/?_r=0

89 Willingham, Emily. "Mercury and Autism Not Linked, Again." *Forbes.com*. Forbes. Web. July 24, 2013. Available at: http://www.forbes.com/sites/emilywillingham/2013/07/24/mercury-and-autism-not-linked-again/

90 United Kingdom. Royal College of Obstetricians and Gynaecologists. "Chemical Exposures During Pregnancy Scientific Impact Paper No. 37." N.a., May 2013. Web.

91 Science Daily. "Repeated Stress in Pregnancy Linked to Children's Behavior." *Sciencedaily.com*. Science Daily. N.a. Web. April 20, 2011. Available at: http://www.sciencedaily.com/releases/2011/04/110420111900.htm

92 Gray, Richard. "Sharing mother's stress in the womb leaves children prone to depression." *Telegraph.co.uk*. The Telegraph. Web. July 14, 2013. Available at: http://www.telegraph.co.uk/science/science-news/10177858/Sharing-mothers-stress-in-the-womb-leaves-children-prone-to-depression.html

93 Poggi, Elysia and Sandman, Curt A. "The Timing of Prenatal Exposure to Maternal Cortisol and Psychosocial Stress is Associated with Human Infant Cognitive Development." *ncbi.nlm.nih.gov*. National Library of Medicine, National Institute of Health. Web. March 26, 2010. Available at: http://www.ncbi.nlm.nih.gov/pmc/articles/PMC2846100/

94 Katarzyna Stolarz-Skrzypek, Jan A. Staessen, et al. for the European Project on Genes in Hypertension (EPOGH) Investigators. "Fatal and Nonfatal Outcomes, Incidence of Hypertension, and Blood Pressure Changes in Relation to Urinary Sodium Excretion." *JAMA*. Journal of the American Medical Association. May 4, 2011, 305(17):1777-1785.

95 Cohen, Hillel W., et al. "Sodium Intake and Mortality in the NHANES II Follow-up Study." *Amjmed.com*. The American Journal of Medicine. March

2006, 119 (3): 275.e7-275.e14. Available at: http://www.amjmed.com/article/S0002-9343(05)01046-6/abstract

96   Moyer, Melinda Wenner. "It's time to end the war on salt." *Scientificamerican.com*. Scientific American. Web. July 8, 2011. Available at: http://www.scientificamerican.com/article.cfm?id=its-time-to-end-the-war-on-salt&page=2

97   Strom, Brian L., et al. "Sodium Intake in Populations: Assessment of the Evidence." *Nap.edu*. National Institute of Medicine. National Academies Press. Web. 2013. Available at: http://www.nap.edu/catalog.php?record_id=18311

98   Ehret, Georg B. "Genetic Variants in Novel Pathways Influence Blood Pressure and Cardiovascular Disease Risk." *Nature.com*. Nature 478.7367 (2011): 103-09. Web. Available at: http://www.nature.com/nature/journal/v478/n7367/abs/nature10405.html#supplementary-information

99   li, Ke., et al. "Interleukin-6 Stimulates Epithelial Sodium Channels In Mouse Cortical Collecting Duct Cells." *ajpregu.physiology.org*. American Journal of Physiology. May 26, 2010. Available at: http://ajpregu.physiology.org/content/early/2010/05/26/ajpregu.00207.2009

100 Bourchard, Chad. "New Salt Study Shakes Up Health Advice." *Indianapublicmedia.org*. Indiana Public Media. Web. September 3, 2013. http://indianapublicmedia.org/eartheats/salt-study-shakes-health-advice/

101 Strom, Brian L., et al. "Sodium Intake in Populations: Assessment of the Evidence." *Nap.edu*. National Institute of Medicine. National Academies Press. Web. 2013. Available at: http://www.nap.edu/catalog.php?record_id=18311

102 Obama, Michelle. "Remarks by the First Lady at the School Nutrition Association Conference." J.W. Marriott Hotel, Washington, D.C. March 1, 2010. Speech.

103 Obama, Michelle. "Press Release: HHS Secretary and Surgeon General Join First Lady to Announce Plans to Combat Overweight and Obesity and Support Healthy Choices." *HHS.gov*. U.S. Department of Health and Human Services. January, 28. 2010.

104 Obama, Michelle. "Press Release: Remarks of First Lady Michelle Obama, Conference of Mayors." *Usmayors.org*. U.S. Conference of Mayors. January 20, 2010. Available at: http://www.usmayors.org/pressreleases/uploads/20100120-speech-obamamichelle.pdf

105 Allan, Mike, "Michelle Obama has new warning on obesity." *Politico.com*. Politico. Web. December 13, 2010. http://www.hhs.gov/news/press/2009pres/07/20090728a.html

106 Sebelius, Kathleen. "Press Release: Secretary Sebelius Addresses CDC Weight of the Nation Conference." *HHS.gov*. U.S. Department of Health and Human Services. Web. July 28, 2009. Available at: http://www.hhs.gov/news/press/2009pres/07/20090728a.html

107 Stein, Robb. "Fewer U.S. Deaths Linked to Obesity." *Washingtonpost.com*. The Washington Post. Web. April 20, 2005. Available at: http://www.washingtonpost.com/wp-dyn/articles/A2929-2005Apr19.html

108 Kasperowicz, Pete. "Dem bill would expand school lunch program to weekends, holidays." *Thehill.com*. The Hill Newspaper. Web. March 25, 2013. Available at: http://thehill.com/blogs/floor-action/house/290147-

dems-propose-expanding-school-lunch-program-to-weekends-holidays#ixzz2d2SW0XK7

109 Share Our Strength. "It's Dinnertime: A Report on Low-Income Families' Efforts to Plan, Shop for and Cook Healthy Meals." N.d. n.a. Available at: http://www.nokidhungry.org/images/cm-study/report-highlights.pdf

110 Obama, Michelle. "Remarks by the First Lady at the School Nutrition Association Conference." J.W. Marriott Hotel, Washington, D.C. March 1, 2010. Speech.

111 Anderson, Sarah E., Ph.D., and Robert C. Whitaker, MD, MPH. "Household Routines and Obesity in US Preschool-Aged Children." *Pediatrics.aappublications.org*. Pediatrics 125.3 (2010): 420-28. American Academy of Pediatrics, 8 Feb. 2010. Web. Available at: http://pediatrics.aappublications.org/content/125/3/420.short

112 USA Today. "Lean beef or pink slime? It's all in a name." Editorial. *Usatoday.com*. USA Today. Web. March 1, 2012.

113 Ibid.

114 Avila, Jim. "Pink Slime and You." *Abcnews.go.com*. ABC News. Web. March 7, 2012. Available at: http://abcnews.go.com/WNT/video/pink-slime-15873068

115 "The 10 worst PR disasters of 2012." *PRdaily.com*. Ragan's PR Daily. Web. December 20, 2012. Available at: http://www.prdaily.com/Main/Articles/The_10_worst_PR_disasters_of_2012_13353.aspx#

116 Hagan, Elisabeth, "Setting the Record Straight on Beef." *Blogs.usda.gov*. U.S. Department of Agriculture Blog. March 22, 2012. Available at: http://blogs.usda.gov/2012/03/22/setting-the-record-straight-on-beef/

117 Donley, Nancy. "In Defense of Food Safety Leadership." *Foodsafetynews.com*. Food Safety News. Web. March 17, 2012.

118 Hungry Wolf, Beverly. "Around the Household." The Ways of My Grandmothers. New York: Quill, 1882. 184+. Print.

119 Densmore, Frances. "Food." Chippewa Customs. St. Paul, MN: Minnesota Historical Society, 1979. 43. Print.

120 Greene, Joel K. Lean Finely Textured Beef: The "Pink Slime" Controversy. CRS Rep. no. R42473. Washington, DC: Library of Congress, Congressional Research Service, 2012. Print.

121 Howard, Philip K. "Why Safe Kids Are Becoming Fat Kids." *Online.wsj.com*. Wall Street Journal. Web. August 13, 2008. Available at: http://online.wsj.com/article/SB121858701285435131.html

122 Ibid.

123 Ibid.

124 Centers for Disease Control and Prevention. "Fire Deaths and Injuries: Fact Sheet." *Cdc.gov*. Centers for Disease Control and Prevention, Home and Recreational Safety. Web. Available at: http://www.cdc.gov/homeandrecreationalsafety/fire-prevention/fires-factsheet.html

125 Israel, Brett, "Airplanes Bear High Levels of Flame Retardants." *Scientificamerican.com*. Scientific American. Web. March 28, 2013. Available at: http://www.scientificamerican.com/article.cfm?id=airplanes-bear-high-levels-of-flame-retardants

126 ibid.
127 Braff, Danielle. "Don't be fooled by paraben hype." *Chicagotribune.com*. The Chicago Tribune. Web. February 16, 2011. Available at: http://articles.chicagotribune.com/2011-02-16/health/sc-health-0216-parabens-20110216_1_paraben-free-phenoxyethanol-shelf-life
128 Gage, Eleni N. "What Are ParabensÐand Do I Need to Worry About Them?" *Realsimple.com*. Real Simple. Web. n.d. Available at: http://www.realsimple.com/beauty-fashion/skincare/worry-about-parabens-00000000028428/index.html
129 U.S. Food and Drug Administration. "Select Committee on GRAS Substances (SCOGS) Opinion: Propyl Paraben." *FDA.gov*. U.S. Food and Drug Administration. Web. April 18, 2013. Available at: http://www.fda.gov/Food/IngredientsPackagingLabeling/GRAS/SCOGS/ucm261033.htm
130 Lovells, Hogan. "EU Scientific Committee on Consumer Safety confirms that parabens in cosmetic products do not pose health risks when used at authorized." *Lexology.com*. Association of Corporate Counsel. Web. July 13, 2013. Available at: http://www.lexology.com/library/detail.aspx?g=120c16d3-3cae-4d3a-9326-8bee2965482e
131 American Cancer Society. "Antiperspirants and Breast Cancer Risk." *Cancer.org*. American Cancer Society. N.a. Web. September 23, 2010. Available at: http://www.cancer.org/cancer/cancercauses/othercarcinogens/athome/antiperspirants-and-breast-cancer-risk?sitearea=MED
132 Jemal, Ahmedin, et al. "Annual Report to the Nation on the Status of Cancer, 1975-2009, Featuring the Burden and Trends in HPV-Associated Cancers and HPV Vaccination Coverage Levels." *Seer.cancer.gov*. U.S. National Institutes of Health, National Cancer Institute. Web. October 19, 2012. Available at: http://seer.cancer.gov/report_to_nation/
133 Braff, Danielle. "Don't be fooled by paraben hype." *Chicagotribune.com*. The Chicago Tribune. Web. February 16, 2011. Available at: http://articles.chicagotribune.com/2011-02-16/health/sc-health-0216-parabens-20110216_1_paraben-free-phenoxyethanol-shelf-life
134 Aveda. "Frequently Asked Questions." Aveda. N.p., n.d. Web. Available at: http://www.aveda.com/cms/customer_service/faq.tmpl#faq18
135 Thomas, Katie. "Johnson & Johnson to Remove Formaldehyde From Products" *nytimes.com*. New York Times. Web. August 15, 2012. Available at: http://www.nytimes.com/2012/08/16/business/johnson-johnson-to-remove-formaldehyde-from-products.html?_r=0
136 Ibid.
137 Karol, Gabrielle. "$315 million price tag on Obamacare menu labeling." *Smallbusiness.foxbusiness.com*. Fox Business Channel. Web. August 22, 2013. http://smallbusiness.foxbusiness.com/entrepreneurs/2013/08/22/315m-price-tag-on-obamacare-menu-labeling/#ixzz2czw0rB5M
138 Doyle, J. Patrick. "On menu regulations, government must do better." *Thehill.com*. The Hill. Web. August 15, 2011. Available at: http://thehill.com/blogs/congress-blog/politics/176887-on-menu-regulations-government-must-do-better#ixzz2d00cz9zx

139 Bream, Shannon. "Supermarkets cry foul as FDA proposes new food labeling rule under ObamaCare." *Foxnews.com*. Fox News. Web. February 6,
2013. Available at: http://www.foxnews.com/politics/2013/02/06/jail-time-
for-food-labels/#ixzz2czvbk0FV

140 Bakalar, Nicholas. "Counting of Calories Isn't Always Accurate." *Nytimes.
com*. The New York Times. Web. January 11, 2010. Available at: http://www.
nytimes.com/2010/01/12/health/12calo.html

141 Stieber, Zachary. "The Cost of Complying with NYC's Soda Ban. *Theepoch-
times.com*. The Epoch Times. Web. February 26, 2013. Available at: http://
www.theepochtimes.com/n2/united-states/the-cost-of-complying-with-
nyc-s-soda-ban-350678.html

142 See Glenn T. Seaborg, Glenn T. "Need We Fear Our Nuclear Future?" *Bulletin
of the Atomic Scientists*, 24, No. 1, 42. January 1968.

143 Conway, Kellyanne. "National Online Survey of Women on 'Alarmism'." The
polling company, inc./WomanTrend. Washington, D.C. May 17, 2013. Web.
Available at: http://iwf.org/files/IWF-Alarmism-Executive-Summary.pdf

144 Gillespie, Nick. "We have deregulated every single aspect of corporate behavior, so that killing people is perfectly legal." *Reason.com*. Reason. Web.
May 3, 2012. Available here: http://reason.com/blog/2012/05/03/we-have-
deregulated-every-single-aspect

145 Momsrising website: http://www.momsrising.org

ABOUT THE AUTHOR

. . . .

Julie Gunlock is the Director of the Culture of Alarmism Project at the Independent Women's Forum. She has written for the New York Post, the Washington Post, the New York Daily News, the Los Angeles Times, Forbes, U.S. News & World Report, The Washington Times, National Review Magazine, National Interest Magazine, the Tampa Tribune, and Townhall.com and is a regular contributor to National Review Online, BlogHer and Huffington Post. She has offered political commentary on Fox News and other networks and is a regular guest on national radio programs. She is married and is a fearless mother to three children.

ABOUT INDEPENDENT WOMEN'S FORUM

. . . .

The Independent Women's Forum is on a mission to expand the conservative coalition, both by increasing the number of women who understand and value the benefits of limited government, personal liberty, and free markets, and by countering those who seek to ever-expand government in the name of protecting women. IWF is a non-partisan, 501(c)(3) research and educational institution. By aggressively seeking earned media, providing easy-to-read, timely publications and commentary, and reaching out to the public, we seek to cultivate support for these important principles and encourage women to join us in working to return the country to limited, Constitutional government.